Published by
Savory Spice Shop
www.savoryspiceshop.com

Authors
Mike and Janet Johnston

Content and recipes by
Stephanie Bullen
Mary Johnston
Mike Johnston
Suzanne Klein
Shantelle C. Stephens
Matt Wallington

Design by
Tony Correa

Photography and food styling by
Tony Correa
Suzanne Klein

Photography contributions by
Kaeli Sandhoff
Artem Nazarov
Susan Kirkpatrick

Copyright © 2014
Savory Franchising Team, LLC

Spice To Plate is a trademark of
Savory Franchising Team, LLC

Library of Congress
Cataloging-in-Publication Data available
ISBN 978-0-9906727-0-8

First Edition - **Printed in Denver, Colorado**

spicetoplate™

30

recipes inspired by

10

signature spice blends

CONTENTS

❧

CONTENTS

PROLOGUE

"Did you ever imagine…?" We hear this a lot when talking with people about Savory Spice Shop. Did we ever imagine that we'd last ten years? That the Savory name would eventually be recognized by more than just our moms? That we'd have owner-operated stores from coast to coast? That we'd still be happily married after running a business together for that long?

The answer is no, the answer is yes. It's one of those things that you don't realize is happening until you stop to reflect on what has happened. We've always followed the philosophy of: taking one day at a time, taking one challenge at a time, celebrating one success at a time, and recognizing one "learning opportunity" at a time. For the last decade, we've tried to do the right thing without paralyzing ourselves with worry about what comes next.

None of this could have happened without the involvement of others: our friends and family whose strong support has been constant, employees who have given so much of themselves and whom we unquestionably trust to "man the ships," allowing us to work on growing the business, and the Savory owner-operators who embrace our concept and continually work to represent Savory in a way that makes us all proud.

And then there are our customers, without whom Savory would be nothing. Without your patronage and loyalty, we would have no reason to continue. You are why we constantly push ourselves to remain innovative. Bringing in new products, creating spice blends, and sharing recipes is what keeps us excited about food and cooking.

So what better time than in the tenth year of business to release our first Savory Spice Shop cookbook? We hope you enjoy reading and cooking from this book as much as we have enjoyed creating it. Whether you have been part of our Savory family for a decade or we've just introduced ourselves, we deeply appreciate your support and continued interest in Savory Spice Shop.

We can only imagine what's next.

Much love,
Mike and Janet Johnston
Founders of Savory Spice Shop

WELCOME

A Cook's Paradise

Walking into a Savory Spice Shop is a sensory delight. Look around and you'll see dozens of shelves stocked with hundreds of sparkling glass jars. The striking burst of red paprikas, bold multihued barbeque blends, and a vibrant wall of green herbs, all neatly organized by category.

The symphony of scents is the next thing our customers notice. For some it's the sweet aroma of baking spices layered over sharp peppercorns or the unmistakably pungent smell of curry. For others it's a hodgepodge, with notes of spicy rubs and earthy seeds drifting across a familiar pantry smell. Scent is a powerful memory trigger and almost everyone seems to have a different description based on the scents they know best.

The sights and scents can be overwhelming the first time you step through the door, but in short order you're greeted by a friendly smile. An apron-clad spice merchant welcomes you warmly, offering to unravel the mysteries of spices and answer your unasked questions.

After sight and smell, two more senses become engaged: touch and taste. Holding the seasoning and feeling the texture inspires many people to take the next step and taste. Some people immediately gravitate to a particular section of the shop. Others bounce from the Taco Seasoning to the cheese blends, then sip water before moving on to taste the Vanilla Bean Sugars and cinnamons.

If you've ever tasted your way through Savory Spice Shop, you know why it's sometimes called "a chef's playground" and "a cook's paradise," stocked nearly floor to ceiling and wall to wall with virtually every herb, spice, and seasoning you can imagine.

The Art of Blending

Shakespeare wrote, "That which we call a rose by any other name would smell as sweet." We think that the same is true for spices. You'll notice that we use the terms blend, seasoning, and spice interchangeably. The American Spice Trade Association defines a spice as, "any dried plant product used primarily for seasoning purposes." We blend seeds, leaves, roots, and flowers to create easy-to-use seasonings. These spice blends can change an ordinary meal into one layered with flavor.

Culinary passion and the magic of inspiration are key components in the art of blending. Our more traditional seasonings are a riff on other cultures' classic combinations or are inspired by a delectable, authentic meal. Some of our signature seasonings transport the taste buds to an exotic locale, and other hand-crafted blends are just happy accidents – the byproduct of an attempt to create something altogether different.

We have always thought that cooking should be fun and believe that a well-balanced seasoning makes a great meal a bit easier and more delicious. While our labels include uses, some customers smell and taste a seasoning, comment on how good it is, then proceed to tell us that they have no idea how they would use it. We have devoted our test kitchen to answering that very question, creating recipes that showcase our signature seasonings. While each recipe in this book was created with a specific blend in mind, we encourage you to "think outside the blend." Use this book not only for the recipes we have created but as inspiration to explore the more versatile but overlooked blends in your pantry.

One Jar Goes Far

The central concept for this book is to showcase ten signature Savory Spice Shop blends, creating three recipes for each. Within the book, you'll find a spectrum of familiar flavors: a curry blend, a mustardy rub, a cheese sprinkle, a smoky barbeque blend, and a baking seasoning.

Creating thirty unique and delicious recipes was a big undertaking, and there had to be rules! First, one jar of the blend had to make all three recipes – to which cookbook contributor Mary Johnston responded with her best infomercial voice, "One jar goes far!" Second, we wanted recipes that weren't too time-consuming and didn't use difficult-to-find ingredients. Finally, we wanted to showcase the blends in different and interesting ways, creating recipes that appeal to a variety of palates.

This was a tall order! Many ideas were considered, recipes created, suggestions made, recipes tweaked, and then made again. We assembled a cross-country panel of volunteer recipe testers: long-time friends of Savory, family members, store owners, employees, and new Savory aficionados. These enthusiastic participants were randomly assigned recipes and asked to make them several times before submitting their reviews. Some recipes were deemed too time-consuming, didn't highlight the blend appropriately, or were delicious but not quite right for this cookbook. As we received feedback, we revisited each dish to make sure we had clear directions and the best selection of recipes.

Spice to Plate

It is often said, "the kitchen is the heart of the home." We couldn't agree more. Few experiences in life are as wonderfully familiar as the pride that comes from creating a beautiful dish: the wafting scent of freshly baked cookies, the sizzle of meat browning on the stove, or the feeling of comfort that comes from sipping a bowl of hot soup. These sights, scents, sounds, and tastes are kitchen experiences that unite people across countries and cultures.

These recipes have been created by people like you: a mother with Mediterranean roots made the comforting Lamb Meatball & Orzo Soup on page 48; a jovial man with an affinity for simple, healthy dishes gave us the Chicken Biryani on page 90; an on-the-go city dweller crafted the barbeque-inspired, vegan Potato Parsnip Soup on page 80; a savvy business owner was inspired by classic French fare and contributed the Parisian Gnocchi on page 66; a woman who has years of culinary experience made a sophisticated dish accessible with the Homemade Gravlax on page 56. Whoever you are, there is a recipe in this book that will speak directly to you.

Spice to Plate is a celebration of flavor intended to inspire you to think about seasonings in a new light. We have organized the book alphabetically by blend, from Baker's Brew Coffee Spice to Zanzibar Curry Powder. Each blend is featured in three recipes, which range from appetizers to main dishes and salads to desserts. These plates will tease your palate and bring a Savory burst of flavor to your kitchen.

In these pages, you'll find elegant dishes, family friendly fare, comfort food, and instant classics. As you cook your way through, enjoy the stories and photos that bring the recipes to life. We hope that *Spice to Plate* becomes one of the dog-eared and stained cookbooks in your kitchen, joining the ranks of the privileged favorites that are pulled out for every occasion.

THE SPICE RACK

Freshness is the key to great flavor. At Savory Spice Shop we grind and blend spices weekly in small batches. Our method of selling in bulk allows customers to keep their spices fresh by purchasing smaller quantities that they will use within the year. In addition to the ten spice blends featured in this cookbook, we layer many recipes with complementary spices to enhance the flavor of the overall dish. Following is a list of the additional spices you'll need to make all of the recipes in the book; plus, these are great basics for your spice rack.

Cayenne: We use cayenne to bring a little heat to the sweet and savory flavors in the Chilean Shepherd's Pie on page 18. Ground cayenne is a 4 to 5 on a heat scale of 1 to 10 and is a must-have for adding a zesty kick to any dish.

Cinnamon: We use ground Saigon cassia cinnamon to add a hint of spiced sweetness to the Festival Fritters on page 96. The flavor of Saigon cassia cinnamon is stronger and sweeter than conventional cinnamon.

Crushed Red Pepper Flakes: Another must-have for adding heat to a dish, we throw these into the Parisian Gnocchi on page 66 and the Festival Fritters on page 96 to give each a mild kick. Red pepper flakes are not a type of chile but rather an assortment of ancho, cayenne, bell peppers, and other chiles.

Cumin: We use ground cumin in the Chilean Shepherd's Pie on page 18 to bring out the savory flavors of the dish and balance the sweetness of the Baker's Brew Coffee Spice. Cumin has an earthy, spiced quality and is used in many global cuisines.

Extracts: Extracts (concentrated flavoring in a neutral alcohol base) are an easy way to elevate or accent existing flavors. We do this with the coconut flavor in the Chocolate Dipped Coconut Macaroons on page 28 by adding coconut extract. We bring out the maple flavor of the Maple Waffles on page 76 by using maple extract. While it will change the end result slightly in both recipes, good old-fashioned vanilla extract can easily be substituted.

Garlic: Easy to use and store, we feature dehydrated garlic in several recipes. Dehydrated minced garlic can be used in place of fresh garlic; 1/8 teaspoon is equal to 1 clove of fresh garlic. In recipes with marinades, sauces, or cooking liquid, it is not necessary to reconstitute before use. We use it in the Creamed Corn Chorizo Spiced Flatbread on page 40, Sausage & Egg Toasty on page 42, Harvest Couscous on page 50, and Parisian Gnocchi on page 66. The garlic featured in our garlic salt is a blend of both granulated and roasted granulated garlic; using both types adds greater depth of flavor. We use garlic salt in the sauce for the Tropical Shrimp Cocktail on page 24.

Ginger: We use ground ginger in the Festival Fritters on page 96. And we use sweetened, crystallized ginger in the Savory Ginger Squares on page 36 and Harvest Couscous on page 50. Ginger has a distinctive sharp flavor that can be used in both sweet and savory dishes.

Lavender: We use lavender as a gorgeous garnish for the Savory Ginger Squares on page 36. This accents the lavender flavor peeking through in the Bohemian Forest European Style Seasoning featured in the recipe.

Mustard Seeds: Yellow mustard seeds are the most common variety and an important ingredient in the dressing for the Chorizo Glazed BBQ Chicken with Bell Pepper Slaw on page 44. While most familiar for their use in the condiment of the same name, we like to toast mustard seeds and add them to sauces and dressings for texture and a tangy punch of flavor.

Paprika: Using smoked paprika in the Roasted Brussels Caesar Salad on page 95 adds great color and a warm and slightly smoky flavor to the dish. To produce smoked paprika, mild, sweet peppers are smoked before being ground.

Onion: Sometimes you want to add onion flavor without the sharp tang of fresh onion. That's when we turn to dehydrated onion. Dehydrated granulated onion adds a subtle layer of onion flavor to the buttery spread in the Sausage & Egg Toasty on page 42. The onion used to create our onion salt is a blend of both granulated and toasted granulated onion; using both adds a sweet yet mild onion flavor to the dressing in the recipe for the Salmon Salad Cakes on page 72.

Peppercorns: When we refer to "coarse ground black pepper" in these recipes, we are using standard Tellicherry black peppercorns. Tellicherry peppercorns can be purchased whole or pre-ground into fine, coarse, extra coarse, or cracked consistencies. Our Four Corners Peppercorn Blend is featured in the Peppercorn & Cheese Crusted Steak on page 68. A blend of black, white, green, and pink peppercorns, each adds a distinctive flavor. Black have the classic pepper flavor, white lend an earthy creaminess, green add a bright sharpness, while pink have a nutty and sweet flavor. (Pink peppercorns are related to cashews and may produce an allergic response in people with allergies to tree nuts.)

Poppy Seeds: We use Dutch blue poppy seeds in the Lemon Poppy Seed Quinoa on page 97 to add color and to complement the nutty flavor of quinoa. While poppy seeds are popular for baking, we love the subtle texture and flavor they lend to savory dishes.

Salt: In these recipes, we use either kosher salt or sea salt. Kosher salt refers to the size of the salt crystal, rather than a specific variety. From baking to marinating, kosher salt is an all-purpose pantry staple. For any recipe calling for sea salt, we use Maldon English Sea Salt. A flake salt with a distinctive pyramid shape, it adds both flavor and texture. It's our go-to sea salt for punching up flavor or as a finishing salt.

Thyme: We use dried thyme to accent the sweet flavors and peppery notes in the Creamed Corn Chorizo Spiced Flatbread on page 40. Closely related to marjoram and oregano, thyme is an aromatic herb with subtle notes of clove and a minty, warm, and peppery flavor.

Tomato Powder: The tangy Chorizo Glazed BBQ Chicken on page 44 and the savory Strawberry BBQ Skewers on page 84 both use tomato powder as a bold, sweet sauce base. Tomato powder mixed with a little water is an easy alternative to using canned paste; 1 tablespoon of powder is equal to 1 tablespoon of paste, or thin as desired for tomato sauce. Tomato powder can also be used to thicken glazes or other sauces.

Wasabi Powder: We use the sweet heat of wasabi (instead of a traditional horseradish) to give the Tropical Shrimp Cocktail on page 24 a unique kick. Wasabi paste is available at most grocery stores, but with powder on hand you can make your own paste just by adding water.

PANTRY STAPLES

This is an overview of standard pantry items, available in any major grocery store, used throughout Spice to Plate. *While the recipes in this book were tested with these items, you may have different staples in your pantry. Substitute according to your tastes, preferences, and dietary needs.*

Oil: The oils we use are canola, coconut, olive, and vegetable. We use all four in various applications, including dressings, sautéing, and frying. When we use the term "olive oil," we are referring to a basic, multi-purpose extra virgin olive oil. Of course, you may choose to substitute with other oils like grapeseed, peanut, or safflower.

Vinegar: We use vinegars that are generally considered basics, including apple cider, balsamic, rice wine, red wine, and white wine. We encourage you to experiment with your favorite flavored and aged vinegars.

Flour: When we list "flour" in a recipe, we are referring to all-purpose flour. This is the only type of flour we use throughout the book.

Sugar: We use white, brown, and confectioners' sugar in these recipes. When we list "sugar" in a recipe, we are referring to granulated white sugar. Recipes using brown sugar will call for either light or dark brown sugar, depending on the flavor and color that is desired. While we use the term "confectioners' sugar," note that some brands may be labeled as powdered sugar. A few of our recipes call for other sweeteners like honey, maple syrup, or molasses.

Butter: Unsalted butter is our staple for both baking and cooking. Many of our seasonings and recipes contain salt, so we find it easiest to start with unsalted butter and add salt when needed.

Broth: For any recipes that call for broth, we define a specific type of broth – typically beef, chicken, or vegetable. In our test kitchen we use bouillon cubes to make broth. For the brands we sell at Savory, one cube plus two cups of water equals two cups of broth. They are flavorful and easy, with less waste than opening cans or boxes of prepackaged broth.

Bread Crumbs: A few recipes call for bread crumbs, used as a binder or to add texture in a batter or topping. The two types of bread crumbs we use are fine, dried bread crumbs and coarser Panko bread crumbs. You can substitute homemade bread crumbs, but we use the easy, prepackaged options available in most grocery stores.

RECEPE GUIDE

❦

Stephanie's Recipe Tasting Notes

Cookbook contributor Stephanie Bullen has been with Savory Spice Shop since 2008, wearing many hats from spice merchant to store manager to franchise trainer. Stephanie's current role, writing about food for Savory, made her the perfect fit for writing and editing the content for *Spice to Plate*. Throughout the process, Stephanie tasted almost every version of each recipe the cookbook crew churned out. Because Stephanie is so familiar with the ten featured spice blends and experienced every recipe in the book, we asked her to share her thoughts about each one. You'll see these in *Stephanie's Recipe Tasting Notes* at the start of each section.

Recipes by Course

The recipes in *Spice to Plate* are organized by seasoning (three recipes for each of the ten featured spice blends), with recipes for three Bonus Side Dishes at the end of the book. We realize that sometimes you may want recipe ideas for a specific course, so below is a guide to help you. Also see *Stephanie's Recipe Tasting Notes*, our recipe testers' quotes at the start of each recipe, or the notes within a recipe for other ideas on how some dishes may work for different courses.

Appetizers
- Tropical Shrimp Cocktail (page 24)
- Scallop Ceviche (page 32)
- Creamed Corn Chorizo Spiced Flatbread (page 40)
- Homemade Gravlax (page 56)
- Dill Pickle Roll Ups (page 64)
- Salmon Salad Cakes (page 72)
- Schnitzel Bites (page 82)

Soups & Salads
- Lamb Meatball & Orzo Soup (page 48)
- Acorn Squash Salad Rounds (page 74)
- Potato Parsnip Soup (page 80)
- Roasted Brussels Caesar Salad (page 95)

Sides
- Caramelized Carrot Risottella (page 34)
- Harvest Couscous (page 50)
- Sweet & Golden Potato Salad (page 58)
- Festival Fritters (page 96)
- Lemon Poppy Seed Quinoa (page 97)

Main Dishes
- Portobello Sandwich (page 16)
- Chilean Shepherd's Pie (page 18)
- Grilled Chicken Lettuce Wraps (page 26)
- Sausage & Egg Toasty (page 42)
- Chorizo Glazed BBQ Chicken (page 44)
- Ham & Asparagus Frittata (page 52)
- French Onion Roast on Toast (page 60)
- Parisian Gnocchi (page 66)
- Peppercorn & Cheese Crusted Steak (page 68)
- Maple Waffles (page 76)
- Strawberry BBQ Skewers (page 84)
- Beer Battered Fish Tacos (page 88)
- Chicken Biryani (page 90)

Desserts
- Salted Caramel Monkey Bread (page 20)
- Chocolate Dipped Coconut Macaroons (page 28)
- Savory Ginger Squares (page 36)
- Mango Coconut Sherbet (page 92)

BAKER'S BREW COFFEE SPICE

14

BAKER'S BREW COFFEE SPICE

Inspired by the aromatic combination of coffee and spices, Baker's Brew contains coffee, sugar, cocoa, cinnamon, salt, nutmeg, cardamom, allspice, mace, and ginger. The flavor is a combination of sweet, bitter, and salty, with just a bit of spiciness from the ginger and nutmeg. That complexity makes it perfect for both decadent baked treats and hearty main dishes.

Stephanie's Recipe Tasting Notes

Portobello Sandwich: Any burger lover will tell you that if you're eating a good one, sauce and juice should drip down your fingers. In that way, this is as much a burger as a sandwich. Napkins are a necessity not a nicety, and the sauces make this recipe exceptional. The reduction is sweet and tangy with hints of coffee and cinnamon, while the aioli is a creamy combination of mustard and garlic. Be generous with the tomato as the sweetness will complement the meaty mushroom. Whether you're a vegetarian or carnivore, this is a seriously good sandwich.

Chilean Shepherd's Pie: While this dish is a bit unusual on paper, it's scrumptious on the plate. I struggled to imagine how briny black olives and sweet raisins would taste with peppery meat and creamed corn, but I was more than willing to give it a try. It's a dish that has the comfort food qualities of a casserole and the flavors of an empanada. I was hooked from the first bite and will be serving this delightful dish on crisp autumn evenings.

Salted Caramel Monkey Bread: Coffee in your coffee cake? Brew a generous pot of coffee, pull cold milk from the fridge, and serve this indulgent, decadent bread to a crowd – otherwise, you might eat the whole pan by yourself! The sugary, crunchy, caramelized crust gives way to soft, chewy bread. While traditional caramel can be fickle, the technique featured here is simple and effective. The sweet, buttery sauce with rich flavors of cocoa and coffee is so good that you just might lick the plate.

Portobello Sandwich with Coffee Aioli

Makes 4 sandwiches

For the mushrooms:

½ cup rice wine vinegar

3 tablespoons soy sauce

2 tablespoons balsamic vinegar

2 tablespoons apricot preserves

1 tablespoon Baker's Brew Coffee Spice

4 large portobello mushrooms

2 tablespoons vegetable oil

1 tablespoon unsalted butter

For the aioli:

1 egg yolk

1 tablespoon Dijon mustard

1 teaspoon rice wine vinegar

1 teaspoon Baker's Brew Coffee Spice

½ teaspoon kosher salt

6 tablespoons vegetable oil

For the sandwich fixings:

4 ciabatta rolls (or other sandwich rolls)

1 to 2 cups spinach leaves

4 thick tomato slices (from 1 tomato)

4 thick slices fresh Mozzarella cheese (from 1 (8-ounce) package)

Raw eggs can carry salmonella bacteria. Use pasteurized eggs if you can find them. If not, make sure your eggs are very fresh (grade A or AA) and properly refrigerated.

For the mushrooms: In a small bowl, whisk rice wine vinegar, soy sauce, and balsamic vinegar with apricot preserves and Baker's Brew. Transfer marinade to a wide baking dish big enough to hold the 4 mushrooms. Remove brown gills from underneath mushroom caps and wipe mushrooms clean. Let mushrooms sit in marinade for 1 to 2 hours at room temperature, flipping once. Heat oil in a large skillet over medium heat. Remove mushrooms from marinade (reserving marinade), set them cap side down in the skillet and cover with a lid. Cook for 2 to 3 minutes then flip and cook, covered, for 2 to 3 more minutes; mushrooms should be slightly tender and have released some of their liquid. Transfer to a plate and cover. Add butter and reserved marinade to the skillet and cook over medium heat until reduced and thick enough to coat the back of a spoon. Remove from heat and reserve as a sauce for the sandwich.

For the aioli: While mushrooms are marinating, prepare the aioli. Add egg yolk, Dijon, vinegar, Baker's Brew, and salt to a blender or small food processor. With blender running, slowly drizzle in oil until aioli reaches a smooth, creamy consistency. Refrigerate until ready to use.

To build the sandwich: Slice rolls in half and toast, if desired. Spread a small spoonful of the reserved mushroom sauce across the bottom half of the roll, then top with a small handful of spinach leaves, a slice of tomato, a slice of cheese, and a mushroom. Spread aioli across the other half of the roll and top the sandwich with it.

"I made the topping and filling a day ahead of time, so the dish came together quickly for an easy weeknight meal. I love the idea of using Baker's Brew in a savory dish; it really works here." ~ Jack Stephens, Oakland, CA

Chilean Shepherd's Pie

Serves 4 to 6

½ cup raisins

1 pound ground beef

1 tablespoon olive oil

1 medium onion, diced

½ cup pitted black olives, sliced

1 tablespoon Baker's Brew Coffee Spice

1 teaspoon ground cumin

¼ teaspoon ground cayenne (optional)

Kosher salt

2 hard boiled eggs, sliced

3 cups corn (drained canned, thawed frozen, or fresh cooked off the cob)

¾ cup heavy cream

½ teaspoon coarse ground black pepper

½ teaspoon sugar

This recipe is based on the traditional Chilean sweet corn casserole, pastel de choclo.

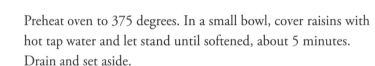

Preheat oven to 375 degrees. In a small bowl, cover raisins with hot tap water and let stand until softened, about 5 minutes. Drain and set aside.

Heat oil in a sauté pan over medium heat; add beef and sauté until browned and cooked through. With a slotted spoon, transfer beef to a bowl. Add onion to pan with beef drippings; cook over medium-high heat, stirring often, until onion is lightly browned, 6 to 8 minutes. Stir in raisins, browned beef, olives, Baker's Brew, cumin, cayenne, and 3 tablespoons water. Reduce heat to medium and cook, stirring frequently, for 3 to 4 minutes. Add salt to taste. Spoon mixture into a 2-quart casserole dish or 8x8 baking dish and top with a layer of sliced hard boiled eggs.

In a food processor, pulse corn, cream, and pepper until coarsely pureed. Rinse and dry the beef sauté pan, then pour corn mixture into the pan. Bring to a simmer over medium heat. Simmer, stirring often, to reduce some of the liquid and until mixture thickens, 5 to 7 minutes. Spoon over beef and eggs to cover, making an even layer. Sprinkle sugar across top of corn mixture.

Set casserole dish on a baking sheet and bake, uncovered, for 30 minutes. For a crispy top, finish under the broiler for 2 minutes or until top is golden brown. (Make sure your casserole dish is broiler-safe.) Let set for 10 minutes before serving.

BAKER'S BREW COFFEE SPICE

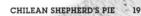

"I served this for Sunday brunch with three generations of family at the table. Our young grandchildren loved the name 'Monkey Bread' and ate it with gusto!" ~ Susan Kirkpatrick, Fort Collins, CO

Salted Caramel Monkey Bread
Serves 6 to 8

2 cups flour, plus more for kneading

1 tablespoon plus 1½ teaspoons Baker's Brew Coffee Spice, divided

4 teaspoons baking powder

¾ teaspoon kosher salt

¼ teaspoon baking soda

12 tablespoons unsalted butter, cold, divided

1 very ripe banana, mashed

¾ cup buttermilk, chilled

½ cup sugar

Cooking spray

½ cup dark brown sugar

1 teaspoon sea salt, divided

This makes a great brunch dish, or serve it with tea or coffee for a sweet breakfast or afternoon snack.

Preheat oven to 350 degrees. In a large mixing bowl, combine flour and 1 tablespoon of the Baker's Brew with baking powder, kosher salt, and baking soda. Using a cheese grater, grate 4 tablespoons of the butter into flour mixture. Use your fingers to mix butter into dry ingredients until the mixture starts to come together. In a separate bowl, whisk banana into buttermilk then pour into dry ingredients. Stir until dough just comes together; it will be very sticky. Turn dough out onto a floured surface, dust top with flour, and gently knead by folding dough over on itself 5 or 6 times. Flatten into a 1-inch thick rectangle, about 4 inches by 6 inches. Cut into 1-inch thick strips and cut strips into 1-inch pieces. (You should end up with 30 to 40 pieces.)

In a gallon-size zip top bag, mix sugar and 1 teaspoon of the Baker's Brew until thoroughly combined. Roll each dough piece into a ball and place in bag with sugar mixture. Once all balls are in the bag, seal and shake until each piece is coated with sugar. Grease an 8- or 9-inch cake or Bundt pan generously with cooking spray. Layer balls evenly in greased pan. Reserve remaining sugar mixture.

In a small saucepan over medium heat, melt remaining 8 tablespoons butter with brown sugar, ½ teaspoon of the sea salt, and remaining ½ teaspoon Baker's Brew, stirring constantly until mixture starts to bubble. Reduce heat to medium-low. Stir continuously until sugar dissolves and mixture thickens into a golden brown caramel sauce, 3 to 5 minutes. ➺

⇢ Pour three-quarters of the caramel sauce over prepared dough balls, reserving the remaining quarter for serving.

Place pan in oven and bake for 35 minutes. Remove from oven and let cool in the pan for at least 20 minutes; don't go too much longer or the caramel will harden in the pan. In the last 5 minutes of cooling, reheat remaining caramel sauce over low heat, stirring, until warm and thin enough to drizzle.

Gently loosen edges of bread from pan with a knife and invert baking pan to release bread onto a serving plate. Drizzle bread with caramel sauce and sprinkle with any remaining sugar mixture and remaining ½ teaspoon sea salt. Set out for people to pull off nuggets of bread with their fingers, or cut into wedges and serve on small plates.

Barrier Reef Caribbean Seasoning (Salt-Free)

The citrus flavor and heat from the chiles in this blend match the bright sun and inviting warmth of the Caribbean to a tee. Barrier Reef is a natural fit with pork or duck. When using this blend we recommend fresh squeezed lime juice as a finishing touch.

1 oz bag -	$2.45	(A)	
4 oz bag -	$5.30	(B)	
16 oz bag -	$17.35	(D)	

2 oz bag -	$3.90 (E)
5 oz bag -	$10.45 (C)

2 floz glass bottle (1.3oz) - $3.95
4 floz glass bottle (2.5oz) - $5.40
12 floz glass bottle (7.6oz) - $11.35

More info on back label

Savory
Spice Shop

Barrier Reef Seaso...

TASTER

BARRIER REEF CARIBBEAN STYLE SEASONING

Inspired by the sweet, warm, citrus flavors of Caribbean cuisine, Barrier Reef contains brown sugar, orange and lemon peel, chiles, ginger, citric acid, nutmeg, mace, cloves, lime leaves, and parsley. The spices in this blend create layers of citrus and heat; the combination of bright lime, tangy lemon, and sweet orange fade into a warm chile flavor.

Stephanie's Recipe Tasting Notes

Grilled Chicken Lettuce Wraps: Preparing these wraps is a hands-on dining experience. First, choose your noodle-to-sauce ratio. The salty, spicy, citrusy sauce will leave you wanting more, so be generous. Add crunchy cucumber and juicy, grilled chicken – just remember to leave enough for everyone else! Finish with sweet mango and zesty scallions. The resulting flavor explosion is totally worth the mess you'll likely make eating them.

Tropical Shrimp Cocktail: This cocktail plays on a perennial party favorite but adds a new medley of flavors. Succulent shrimp absorbs the spicy citrus sauce, sweet pineapple offsets the heat, and cabbage provides a refreshing crunch. It's a fairly simple dish to make (despite having several layers) and is a great party appetizer. The combination of sauce and shrimp is great on its own, but the complete dish is well worth the extra effort.

Chocolate Dipped Coconut Macaroons: These were a pleasant surprise, as coconut has never been my favorite flavor. Crisp coconut flakes kissed with bright citrus and slight heat create a delightful dessert. Smooth chocolate and curls of zest top off this two-bite treat. White chocolate and lime is mild and sweet, while dark chocolate and orange is rich and bold. These are perfect paired with coffee or a cocktail. Be forewarned – it's nearly impossible to have just one!

"This dish makes me yearn for summer and a beach. I love shrimp and pineapple and this is different than any other cocktail sauce I've ever had. For a party-style serving, I would just make the cocktail sauce to serve as a dip with shrimp." ~ Lia Moran, Denver, CO

Tropical Shrimp Cocktail
Serves 4 to 6

For the cocktail sauce:

1 cup ketchup

1 tangerine, zest grated and juiced

1 tablespoon freshly grated ginger (from about a 3-inch piece)

½ teaspoon Worcestershire sauce

1 tablespoon Barrier Reef Caribbean Style Seasoning

½ teaspoon garlic salt

½ teaspoon wasabi powder (or 1 teaspoon prepared wasabi paste)

To build the shrimp cocktail:

2 cups shredded cabbage

½ cup chopped fresh cilantro

½ lime, zest grated and juiced

1 pound cooked jumbo shrimp (16 to 20), with tails

1 cup diced fresh pineapple (about ½ small pineapple)

Orange zest and juice can be used in place of tangerine. Adjust wasabi to taste, adding more for additional heat.

For the cocktail sauce: In a small bowl, combine ketchup with ½ teaspoon of the tangerine zest and 2 tablespoons of the tangerine juice. Whisk in ginger, Worcestershire, Barrier Reef, garlic salt, and wasabi powder. Cover and refrigerate for at least 2 hours or up to overnight. The longer it sits, the more the flavors will develop.

To build the shrimp cocktail: Toss cabbage and cilantro with the lime zest and juice. Set aside 1 to 2 whole shrimp to garnish each serving. Peel the rest of the shrimp, chop into bite-size pieces and mix with the diced pineapple. In a martini glass or ice cream dish, build the cocktail by the spoonful in the following layers: cocktail sauce, cabbage mixture, shrimp mixture, cocktail sauce. Repeat those layers depending on the size of your serving glass. Peel the reserved whole shrimp, leaving the tails in tact, and use them to garnish each serving.

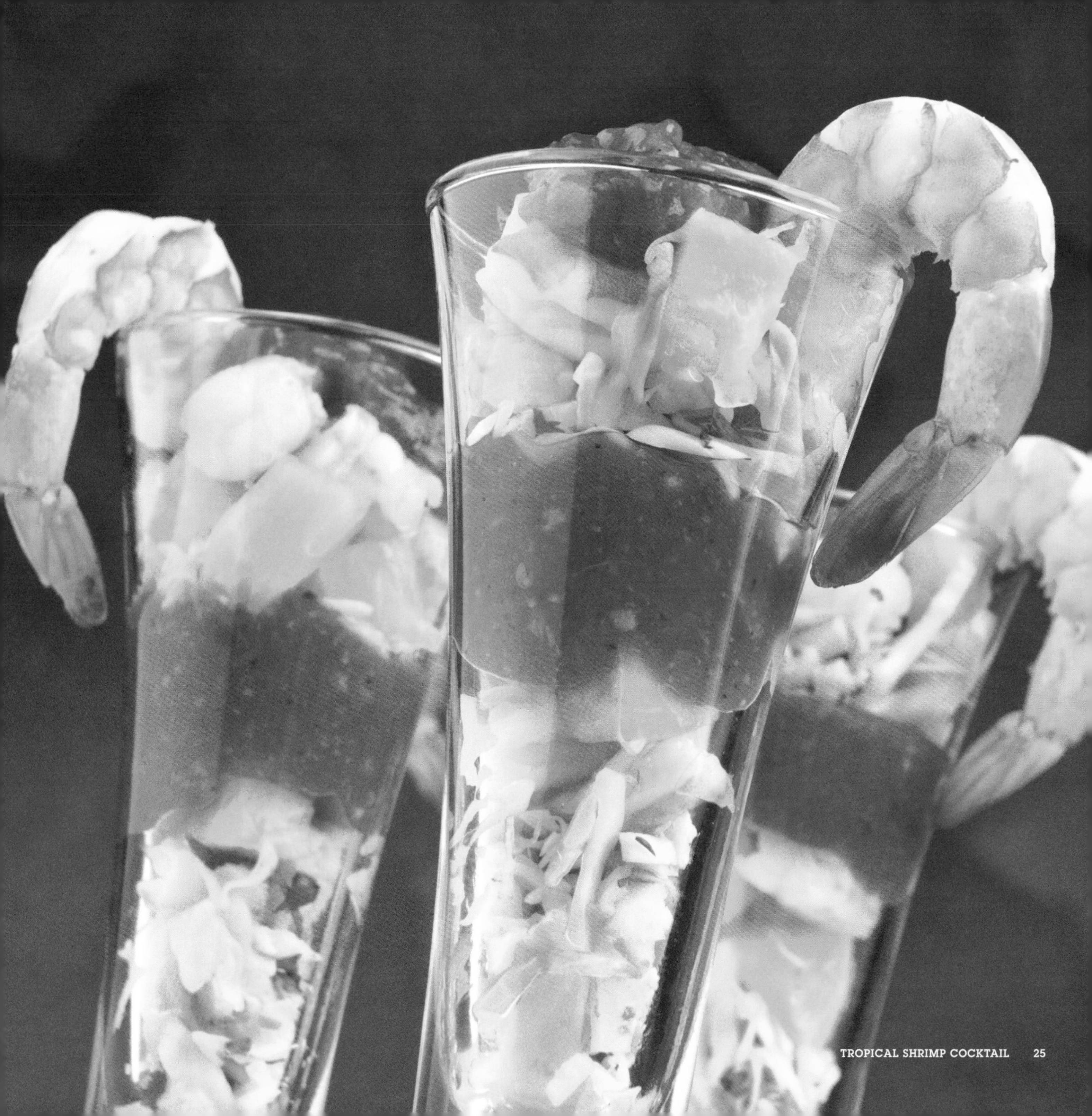

Grilled Chicken Lettuce Wraps

Serves 4 to 6

- ⅓ **cup soy sauce**
- ⅓ **cup fish sauce**
- **3 tablespoons mirin (sweet rice cooking wine)**
- **3 tablespoons honey**
- **2 tablespoons Barrier Reef Caribbean Style Seasoning**
- **1½ pounds boneless, skinless chicken thighs or breasts**
- **4 ounces very thin rice sticks (also called Maifun rice noodles)**
- **1 head Bibb (or Boston) lettuce, whole leaves plucked, rinsed, and dried**
- **1 mango, peeled, pitted, and diced**
- **½ cucumber, quartered lengthwise and thinly sliced**
- **4 scallions, white and green parts sliced**
- **½ cup chopped peanuts (optional)**

Mirin can be found in most grocery stores alongside other Asian pantry products.

For the sauce: Whisk together soy sauce, fish sauce, mirin, honey, and Barrier Reef until honey is incorporated. Place chicken in a zip top storage bag. Pour half of the sauce over chicken, seal bag and refrigerate for at least 30 minutes or up to 2 hours. Reserve remaining sauce.

For the chicken: Preheat grill to medium-high, making sure it is well oiled. Remove chicken from refrigerator and shake off any excess marinade. Grill until cooked through, 10 to 20 minutes depending on grill heat and size of chicken. Turn chicken over halfway through to get an even char on all pieces. (The chicken can also be pan seared on the stovetop over medium-high heat with a little canola oil.) Remove chicken from grill and mince into small pieces. Transfer to a serving bowl and toss with 1 to 2 tablespoons of the reserved sauce.

For the garnishes and to serve: Place noodles in a medium saucepan or heatproof bowl and cover with boiling water. Steep for 10 minutes or until noodles are soft. Drain, rinse with cold water, transfer to a serving bowl and toss with 1 to 2 tablespoons of the reserved sauce. Stack lettuce leaves on a serving plate. Place remaining reserved sauce, mango, cucumber, scallions, and peanuts in separate serving bowls. Serve family-style so everyone can assemble to taste. Build a wrap starting with 1 lettuce leaf topped with a small pile of noodles. Add a scoop of chicken and scatter remaining garnishes on top to taste. Serve with extra sauce.

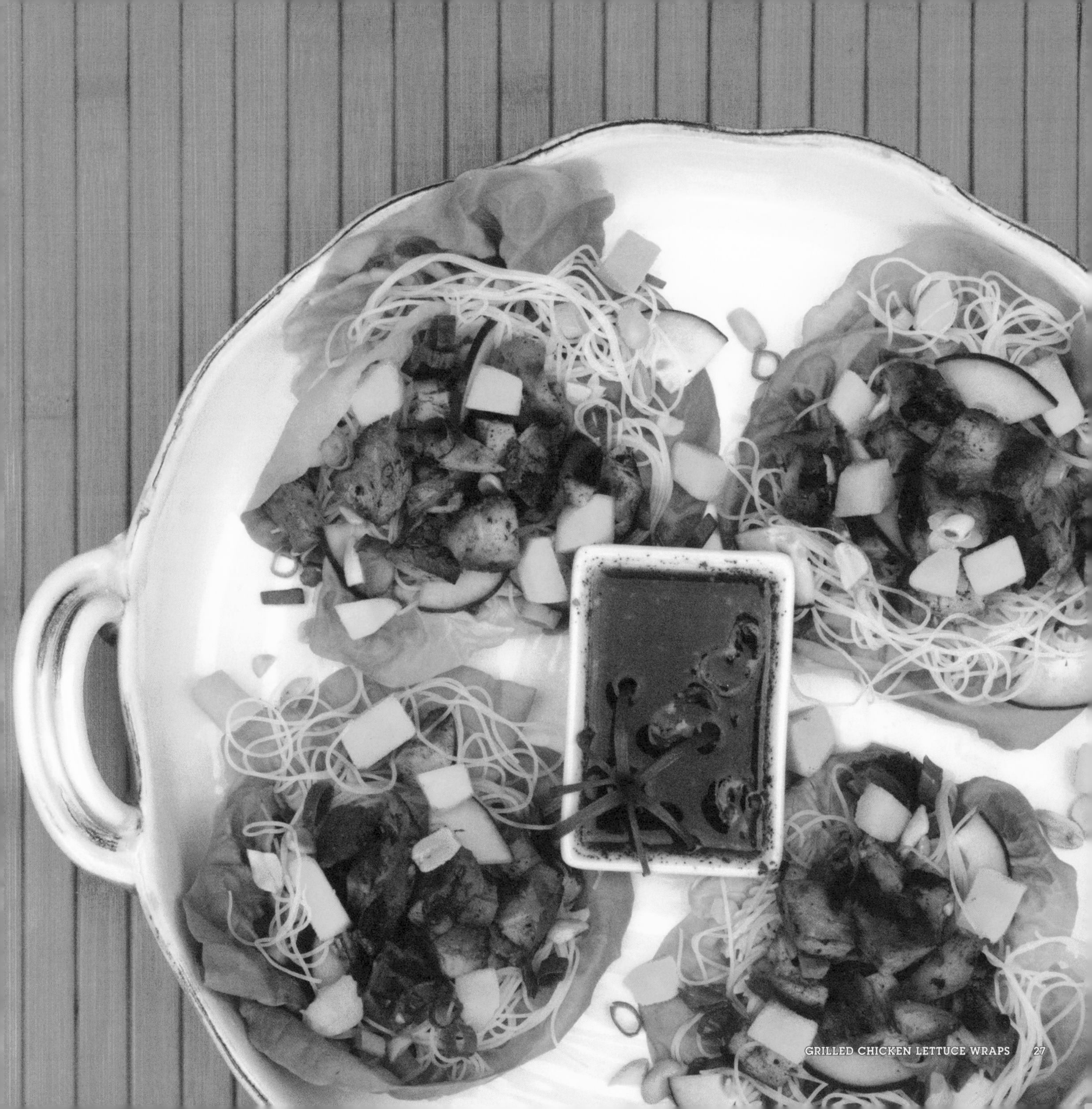

Chocolate Dipped Coconut Macaroons

Makes 22 to 26 macaroons

3 egg whites

4 teaspoons Barrier Reef Caribbean Style Seasoning

1 teaspoon coconut or vanilla extract

1 (14-ounce) package sweetened shredded coconut (about 4 cups)

¼ cup sugar

½ teaspoon sea salt

¾ cup white or dark chocolate chips

1 lime or small orange, zest grated

Pair white chocolate with lime zest or dark chocolate with orange zest depending on your flavor preference. These will keep for a few days at room temperature in an airtight container.

Combine egg whites, Barrier Reef, and extract in a small bowl and let sit for 15 minutes at room temperature. Preheat oven to 350 degrees and line 2 baking sheets with parchment paper.

Add coconut, sugar, salt, and egg white mixture to the bowl of a food processor. Process until ingredients come together in a uniform texture, 15 to 30 seconds. (Alternatively, mix ingredients together by hand; final macaroons won't be as smooth in texture with this method.)

Firmly pack a tablespoon-sized scoop with the mixture to form a mound. Carefully tap the scoop onto the prepared baking sheet to release the mound. (It helps to lightly wet your fingers and the scoop each time to prevent too much sticking.) Repeat with remaining mixture. Using wet fingers, clean up mounds so they are smooth and neat. Bake for 15 to 20 minutes or until golden brown at the base and slightly firm to the touch. Let macaroons cool on the baking sheet; they will firm up while cooling.

Once macaroons are completely cool, melt chocolate chips in the microwave on high for 30 seconds. Stir with a spatula then microwave for another 30 seconds or until chocolate is mostly melted. Stir with the spatula again until any remaining chocolate bits are completely melted and smooth. (Alternatively, melt chips in a double boiler over simmering water.) ⇢

⇢ Holding each macaroon at its base, swirl the top third of the macaroon into the melted chocolate and place it back on the baking sheet. Let chocolate cool for at least 5 minutes then sprinkle each macaroon with lime or orange zest. Let chocolate set completely before serving, 30 minutes to 1 hour.

Savory
Spice Shop®

Bohemian Forest European
Seasoning

Purchase
Date:
6295 S. Main St., Aurora, CO · (303) 680-211
www.savoryspiceshop.com

Net
Weight:

BOHEMIAN FOREST EUROPEAN STYLE SEASONING

Inspired by hearty Central European cuisine, Bohemian Forest contains crushed brown mustard, garlic, rosemary, pepper, thyme, savory, parsley, lavender, and sage. Sharp mustard is offset by a medley of savory herbs and sweet lavender. Cooking with this blend allows the spices to release their full volatile or essential oils and results in a comforting infusion of flavor.

Stephanie's Recipe Tasting Notes

Scallop Ceviche: Buttery scallops are highlighted by this earthy herb and mustard seasoning. The additional ingredients add a Mediterranean flair. Briny olives and salty capers balance the tang of citrus, while the burst of grape tomatoes lends a sweetness that's tempered by fresh chiles. The corn chips are essential and will change the way you think about tortilla chips. Almost cracker-like, they easily hold the weight of the ceviche (or any other dip you pile on) and add a perfect finishing dash of salt and pepper to each bite.

Caramelized Carrot Risotella: This dish marries two classic comfort foods: risotto (laborious) and paella (time-consuming). This recipe is easier and quicker to prepare, while maintaining the comfort food qualities of both. The sharp, slightly bitter flavor of brown mustard seeds adds dimension to the sweet flavor of cooked carrots and shallots. The end result is creamy but not heavy. Finally, a sprinkling of parsley adds freshness. This easy-to-make dish, like a warm blanket, is the perfect thing to curl up with on a cool evening.

Savory Ginger Squares: Naming this delicious bite was a struggle. Too savory to be a gingersnap, too chewy and sweet to be a cracker, we settled on calling them "squares." If you want an excuse to eat a cookie as an appetizer, this is it! Mustard and aromatic herbs are offset by molasses and sweet brown sugar. Pair this ginger square with cheese and fruit for the perfect pre-meal bite. Serve it as dessert by adding ice cream and a bit of the leftover glaze. Add a robust red wine and serve it with a dessert-style cheese plate.

Scallop Ceviche with Salt and Pepper Corn Chips
Serves 4 to 6

For the ceviche:

12 to 16 ounces fresh or frozen sea scallops

¾ cup lime juice, freshly squeezed (6 to 8 limes)

¼ cup lemon juice, freshly squeezed (1 to 2 lemons)

1 jalapeño chile, seeded and diced

1 tablespoon balsamic vinegar

1 tablespoon fish sauce

1½ tablespoons Bohemian Forest European Style Seasoning

¼ cup olive oil

1 cup grape or cherry tomatoes, halved and seeded

1 medium red onion, large dice

1 ripe avocado, large dice

½ cup chopped fresh cilantro

¼ cup capers, drained

¼ cup sliced Spanish olives

For the corn chips:

6 (6-inch) corn tortillas

¼ cup coconut oil, melted

¾ teaspoon coarse ground black pepper

½ teaspoon kosher salt

Shrimp can be used in place of scallops, or try a combination of both.

For the ceviche: If using frozen scallops, defrost first. Rinse scallops and pat dry with paper towel. Cut into bite-size pieces; halve or quarter if large. In a large, non-reactive bowl, mix scallops, lime and lemon juices, jalapeño, vinegar, fish sauce, and Bohemian Forest. Cover and refrigerate for a minimum of 3 hours or up to overnight. (The scallops will be "cooking" in the marinade and will be "done" when they become opaque.) Gently fold in olive oil, tomatoes, onion, avocado, cilantro, capers, and olives. Cover and return to refrigerator to marinate another hour.

For the corn chips: While ceviche finishes marinating, preheat oven to 375 degrees and line a baking sheet with parchment paper. Stack tortillas, wrap in a damp paper towel and microwave on high for 1 minute to soften. Cut tortillas into triangles or thick wedges and toss with coconut oil, pepper, and salt until coated. Lay tortilla pieces in a single layer on the baking sheet. Bake until golden brown and crisp, 8 to 10 minutes, flipping over halfway through. Watch carefully, you want them to just crisp. Remove from oven and cool on baking sheet.

To serve: Use a slotted spoon to scoop out ceviche into small bowls. Serve with salt and pepper corn chips.

"This is such a colorful and simple dish. I like the play on a faux risotto, plus it's easier to make than a traditional risotto. Bohemian Forest is the perfect spice complement to this recipe. I can see serving it as a side with chicken, pork, fish, or lamb." ~ Stephanie Birn, San Diego, CA

Caramelized Carrot Risottella

Serves 4 to 6

1 tablespoon olive oil

2 tablespoons unsalted butter

3 to 4 medium carrots, small dice (about 2 cups)

3 large shallots, small dice (about 1½ cups)

1½ teaspoons kosher salt, plus more for seasoning

1 teaspoon sugar

1½ tablespoons Bohemian Forest European Style Seasoning

1 cup Arborio rice

¾ cup dry, crisp white wine (e.g. Pinot Grigio)

3 cups vegetable or chicken broth

¼ cup mascarpone cheese

¼ cup roughly chopped flat-leaf parsley

To punch up the paella qualities of this dish, add ¼ to ½ teaspoon saffron with the broth.

In a wide, heavy-bottomed pot with a lid, heat olive oil and butter over medium-high until they begin to brown. (The butter will foam and turn from pale yellow to light brown; watch carefully to avoid burning.)

Stir in carrots and shallots. Sprinkle with salt, sugar, and Bohemian Forest. Continue to cook over medium-high heat, uncovered, stirring occasionally, until vegetables begin to soften and caramelize, about 10 minutes. (Both carrots and shallots should have lots of browned spots.)

Stir in rice and combine thoroughly with vegetable mixture. Cook for 3 more minutes, stirring frequently. Stir in wine and cook until wine evaporates completely, 3 to 5 minutes. Stir in broth, bring to a boil then reduce to a low simmer. Cover pot with lid and cook for 20 minutes or until liquid is absorbed and rice is tender. Remove from heat and stir in mascarpone. Season with additional salt to taste. (For additional texture, crisp the bottom of the rice by putting the pot back on the stovetop over medium-high heat, uncovered, for 4 to 8 minutes.) Sprinkle with parsley and serve warm.

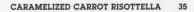

*"These are lovely and delicious…like a savory, chewy adult gingerbread.
They are very creative for a dinner party, especially to accompany something
more savory like a cheese plate."* ~ Kerry Brown, Atlanta, GA

Savory Ginger Squares

Makes 18 to 24 squares

5 tablespoons unsalted
   butter, softened

⅔ cup dark brown sugar

⅓ cup molasses

2 eggs, 1 whole and 1 with
   yolk and white separated

2 tablespoons Bohemian Forest
   European Style Seasoning

1 tablespoon baking soda

1 teaspoon kosher salt

3 cups flour, plus more for
   rolling dough

2 tablespoons water

1 teaspoon grated lemon zest

1 teaspoon grated orange zest

1 cup diced crystallized
   ginger, divided

2 tablespoons lemon juice

1 cup confectioners' sugar

1 tablespoon lavender

*Instead of rolling and cutting
the dough into squares or
other shapes, you can turn
them into tablespoon sized
drop cookies; the baking time
will remain the same.*

Preheat oven to 350 degrees and line 2 baking sheets with parchment paper. In a stand mixer, cream butter with brown sugar and molasses on high speed until incorporated, about 1 minute. Lower speed to medium, add 1 whole egg and mix until incorporated. Add egg yolk and continue mixing until incorporated; scrape down the sides of the bowl as necessary. Add Bohemian Forest, baking soda, salt, and half of the flour. Mix at medium speed until incorporated, scraping down the sides of the bowl again if necessary. Add water, lemon and orange zest, ¾ cup of the diced crystallized ginger, and remaining half of the flour and mix until dough just comes together.

Turn dough out onto a floured surface and knead for a minute until a smooth ball comes together. Divide dough in half and roll out each half into a ½-inch thick square. Cut dough into 2-inch squares or diamonds, or use a cookie cutter shape of your choice. Place squares about 1 inch apart on the prepared baking sheets.

Whisk egg white with lemon juice and confectioners' sugar. Using a pastry brush, brush a thin layer of glaze on each square. (For a nice crackle affect, glaze squares just before they go in the oven. You'll likely end up with leftover glaze.) Top each square with 2 to 3 pieces of the remaining diced crystallized ginger and sprinkle with lavender to taste. Bake one sheet at a time for 5 minutes then turn the sheet around in the oven and bake for 5 more minutes. Let squares cool on the baking sheets before serving. These will keep for up to 3 days stored in an airtight container.

BOHEMIAN FOREST EUROPEAN STYLE SEASONING

CHIMAYO CHORIZO SAUSAGE SPICE

CHIMAYO CHORIZO SAUSAGE SPICE

Inspired by and named after Mexican sausage, Chimayo Chorizo contains chiles, salt, sugar, oregano, cumin, garlic, and pepper. The sharp heat of chiles in this blend is grounded by earthy oregano and cumin, subtle sweetness, and a hint of salt.

Stephanie's Recipe Tasting Notes

Creamed Corn Chorizo Spiced Flatbread: Growing up, I loved roasted tomatoes stuffed with corn and topped with bread crumbs. This delightful recipe elevates that dish. Flavorful chorizo infused flatbread, thick enough for ample toppings, may become your go-to recipe for pizza crust or other flatbreads. Creamy cheese and sweet corn are the perfect foil for the spicy seasoning, while fire roasted tomatoes add sweetness. Warm leftovers in the oven and top with a fried egg for a hearty breakfast. This recipe yields three medium flatbreads, but you can easily divide the dough to make individual servings.

Sausage & Egg Toasty: This toasty will make you forget the blasphemy of lackluster breakfast sandwiches with cardboard muffins, flavorless meat, and rubbery eggs. The recipe features freshly toasted English muffins and a flavorful, slightly spicy sausage. A perfectly fried egg cuts the heat, as does the cooling herbed queso. You might want to keep a jar of the herbed queso on hand so you can add this refreshing spread to sandwiches, pasta, or omelets. Hearty enough to be a weekend brunch or the star of "breakfast for dinner" nights, these basic components add up to a toasty, or breakfast sandwich, to which all others aspire.

Chorizo Glazed BBQ Chicken: Barbeque chicken and slaw belong together like peanut butter and jelly or cheese and crackers. The marinade gives the chicken a sweet heat that is finger licking good. The slaw is a refreshing accompaniment that rests in the refrigerator while you grill the chicken. Festival Fritters (one of our Bonus Side Dish recipes) are sweet bites of dough that complete the meal. Together, a perfect summer barbeque.

"This is a fun dish for a backyard party. I would prep the components ahead of time and refrigerate them. You could reheat the toppings while you roll out the dough. That way, you could assemble, grill, and eat in less than 10 minutes." ~ Dan Hayward, Boulder, CO

Creamed Corn Chorizo Spiced Flatbread

Makes 3 medium flatbreads

1 cup warm water

2 packages active dry yeast
(or 4½ teaspoons)

¼ cup apple cider vinegar

1 tablespoon Worcestershire sauce

1 lime, zest grated and juiced

1 tablespoon light brown sugar

½ teaspoon dehydrated minced garlic
(or 4 cloves garlic, minced)

3 tablespoons plus 2 teaspoons
olive oil, divided

2 teaspoons kosher salt,
plus more for seasoning

2 tablespoons Chimayo Chorizo Sausage
Spice, plus more for sprinkling

4 cups flour, plus more for rolling dough

4 ears corn, shucked and rinsed

3 plum tomatoes, halved lengthwise

1 large shallot, diced (about ½ cup)

¾ cup heavy cream

½ cup vegetable broth

¼ teaspoon dried thyme

Coarse ground black pepper
for seasoning

½ cup shredded Mozzarella cheese

2 tablespoons shredded
Parmesan cheese

¼ cup chopped fresh cilantro

For the dough: In the bowl of a stand mixer, combine water and yeast. Let stand for 10 minutes or until yeast activates and starts to foam. Add vinegar, Worcestershire, and 1 tablespoon of the lime juice. Stir in brown sugar and garlic until yeast and sugar are dissolved. Fit mixer with the dough hook, turn on low and add 2 tablespoons of the oil, 2 teaspoons of the salt, and 2 tablespoons of the Chimayo Chorizo. Add the flour ½ cup at a time until dough forms. Increase speed to medium and continue mixing for an additional 5 minutes. Stop the mixer as needed to scrape dough off the hook. Turn dough out onto a lightly floured surface and form into a ball. Lightly oil a large bowl with 1 teaspoon of the oil; add dough and turn to coat it with oil. Cover with a damp towel and let dough rise in a warm spot (about 85 degrees, over a gas pilot light or near a warm oven) until doubled in size, about 1 hour. Divide dough into three smaller balls and return to bowl. Cover and let rise again for 30 minutes.

For the toppings: In a large stockpot, bring 2 quarts of water to a boil. Add corn and boil for 10 minutes; drain and set aside. While corn cooks, lightly oil grill and preheat to medium-high. Toss tomato halves with 1 teaspoon of the oil and a few sprinkles of Chimayo Chorizo. Place tomatoes on grill flesh side down and cook for 4 to 5 minutes; turn and repeat on skin side. Remove from grill, let cool and slice into ¼-inch pieces. While tomatoes cool, place boiled corn on grill for 1 to 2 minutes per "side," ⇒

CHIMAYO CHORIZO SAUSAGE SPICE

40

⇢ adjusting by ¼ turn every couple of minutes so corn chars somewhat evenly. Remove from grill, let cool and cut roasted kernels from cobs. Heat remaining 1 tablespoon oil in a large sauté pan over medium-high heat. Add shallots and cook until translucent, 3 to 5 minutes. Stir in corn kernels, cream, broth, thyme, and lime zest. Season with salt and pepper to taste. Bring to a simmer and cook for 10 minutes, stirring occasionally. Stir in both cheeses, remove from heat and cover until ready to assemble.

To assemble: Roll out each dough ball on a floured surface to about ¼-inch thick and place on lightly oiled grill over medium-high heat. Grill for about 1 to 2 minutes per side. Top each flatbread with warm creamed corn and tomato pieces. Return to grill and cook for 2 to 3 more minutes. Remove from grill, sprinkle with Chimayo Chorizo and top with cilantro. Slice and serve warm.

"I've used Chimayo Chorizo many times, but pairing it with the sun-dried tomatoes is amazing. I grow mint, sage, and tomatillos in my garden, so this will be one of those go-to recipes for me. And I would make the patties and spread the night before to save on breakfast prep time." ~ Brooke Franklin, Littleton, CO

Sausage & Egg Toasty with Herbed Queso Spread
Makes 4 toasty sandwiches

½ pound ground pork

¼ cup diced sun-dried tomatoes

2 tablespoons Chimayo Chorizo
 Sausage Spice

1 tablespoon apple cider vinegar

1½ teaspoons water

1 medium tomatillo,
 husked and rinsed

½ cup packed fresh mint leaves

½ cup packed fresh sage leaves

2 scallions, white and
 green parts sliced

¼ cup pine nuts

½ teaspoon dehydrated minced garlic
 (or 4 cloves garlic, minced)

½ cup diced queso fresco

1 tablespoon olive oil

2 teaspoons lime juice

Kosher salt and coarse ground
 black pepper

4 tablespoons unsalted
 butter, softened

½ teaspoon dehydrated
 granulated onion

4 English muffins

4 eggs

For the sausage: Mix pork with diced sun-dried tomatoes, Chimayo Chorizo, vinegar, and water. Form into four patties, about the size of an English muffin. Cover and refrigerate for 30 minutes or up to overnight. Remove patties from refrigerator and bring to room temperature when ready to assemble.

For the spread: Preheat broiler. Place tomatillo on a baking sheet and broil until blistered and charred, 7 to 12 minutes, turning halfway through. Set aside to cool. In a food processor, pulse roasted tomatillo, mint, sage, scallions, pine nuts, garlic, and queso fresco to combine. Slowly add oil and lime juice until incorporated; mixture should be paste-like. Season with salt and pepper to taste. Refrigerate until ready to assemble.

To assemble the toasty sandwiches: Preheat oven to 225 degrees. Thoroughly combine butter and granulated onion; spread mixture on the inside of each English muffin. Lay muffins butter-side up on a baking sheet and toast in oven until golden, about 18 to 20 minutes. Meanwhile, in a medium skillet over medium heat, cook sausage patties until browned and cooked through, flipping halfway, 10 to 12 minutes. Remove patties from skillet and blot with paper towel to remove excess grease; tent with foil to keep warm. Meanwhile, in a medium nonstick skillet over medium heat, fry eggs to desired doneness. Remove from heat and season with salt and pepper to taste. Cover to keep warm. ⇒

→ Build each toasty by slathering a generous amount of herbed queso spread on the bottom muffin slice, then top with sausage and fried egg. Finish with the top muffin slice. Serve warm.

"Perfect for a Saturday night barbeque! It's so easy, especially if you prep the glaze and slaw ahead of time. The glaze has nice heat without being overwhelming, and the slaw dressing has a nice zing." ~ Kathy VanPeursem, Denver, CO

Chorizo Glazed BBQ Chicken with Bell Pepper Slaw
Serves 6 to 8

12 chicken drumsticks

Kosher salt and coarse ground black pepper

2 tablespoons Chimayo Chorizo Sausage Spice

1 tablespoon tomato powder (or 2 tablespoons tomato paste)

4 tablespoons apple cider vinegar, divided

5 tablespoons water, divided

2½ tablespoons honey, divided

2 teaspoons yellow mustard seeds

3 tablespoons Dijon mustard

2 tablespoons mayonnaise

1 tablespoon olive oil

4 (4-inch) sprigs rosemary, leaves removed and finely chopped

1 small lemon, zest grated

3 red bell peppers, thinly sliced into 2-inch strips

½ head green cabbage, thinly sliced then roughly chopped

1 stalk celery, cut into ⅛-inch slices

2 scallions, white and green parts sliced thinly on the bias

Serve with the Festival Fritters on page 96.

For the chicken: Cut three 1-inch slits through skin into flesh of each drumstick and sprinkle with a few pinches of salt and pepper. In a large bowl, prepare glaze by mixing Chimayo Chorizo, tomato powder (or paste), 2 tablespoons of the vinegar, 3 tablespoons of the water, and 1½ tablespoons of the honey. In a small bowl, mix 2 tablespoons of the glaze with remaining 2 tablespoons water and set aside for basting. Add drumsticks to the large bowl of glaze and toss to coat. Cover and refrigerate for 30 minutes or up to 1 hour. Preheat grill to medium-high and remove drumsticks from refrigerator to bring to room temperature. Grill drumsticks on each of their 4 rounded sides, turning every 7 to 8 minutes and lightly basting with reserved glaze after each turn. (Internal temperature of finished drumsticks should be 170 to 175 degrees.) Let rest, covered, for 10 minutes before serving.

For the slaw: While chicken is marinating, toast mustard seeds over medium-high heat in a small skillet until aromatic and lightly browned, 2 to 5 minutes. Stir often to prevent burning; transfer to a small dish to cool. Prepare dressing in a large bowl by whisking remaining 2 tablespoons vinegar and remaining 1 tablespoon honey with mustard, mayonnaise, oil, rosemary, lemon zest, and the cooled mustard seeds. Add bell peppers, cabbage, celery, and scallions to the dressing and toss until fully coated. Cover and refrigerate for at least 30 minutes. Serve cold or at room temperature alongside the glazed BBQ chicken.

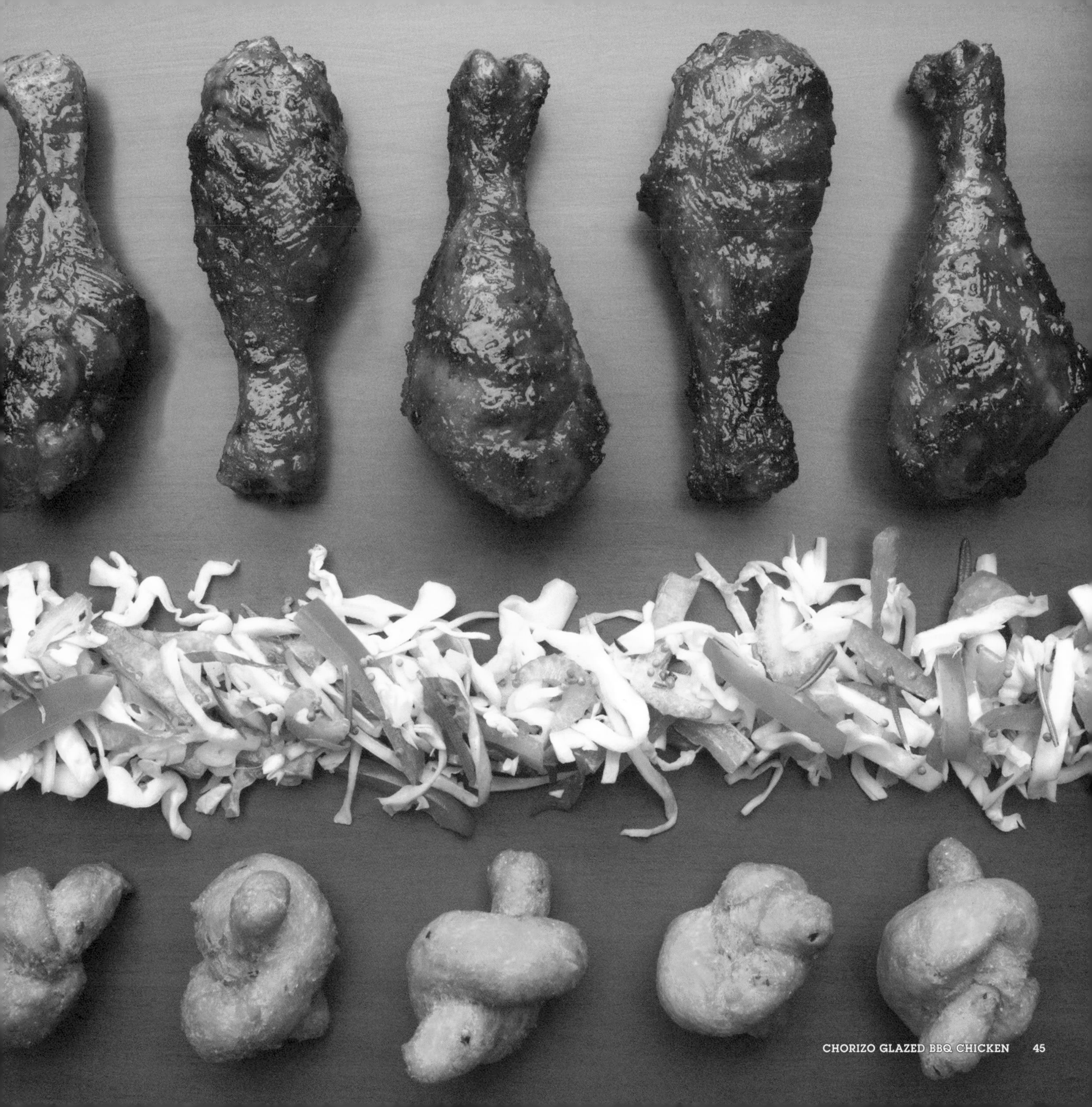

Savory
Spice Shop®

Hidden Cove Lemon Garlic
Blend

Purchase
Date:

Net
Weight:

www.savoryspiceshop.com

HIDDEN COVE LEMON GARLIC BLEND

Inspired by Caribbean island spices, Hidden Cove contains lemon peel, garlic, salt, ginger, onion, allspice, parsley, white pepper, sugar, fenugreek, turmeric, mace, black pepper, thyme, coriander, cumin, cayenne, arrowroot, cinnamon, anise, cloves, and cardamom. This combination of unique and familiar ingredients has become a customer favorite.

Stephanie's Recipe Tasting Notes

Lamb Meatball & Orzo Soup: Nothing says comfort food like chicken noodle soup…and this take on a childhood favorite will please even the most sophisticated palate. This simple soup is more than the sum of its parts: hearty roasted meatballs, bits of pasta swimming in broth, the soft crunch of carrot, and vibrant spinach leaves. Fresh ingredients make this perfect for both the warmer days of spring and those frosty winter nights.

Harvest Couscous: Not too sweet and not too savory, Goldilocks would call this recipe "just right." Sweet fruits balance the savory flavors of shallot and garlic. Refreshing mint and tangy dried cherries shine in this dish. Easily made ahead, it's good at room temperature or straight from the fridge. A surefire crowd pleaser, whether for a summer potluck or autumn brunch, this will be my contribution to many future gatherings.

Ham & Asparagus Frittata: I've never understood why anyone would mix ham and pineapple – this dish, incredibly, made me a believer. The frittata is good on its own but something almost magical happens when you add the sauce. The eggs take on the tang of crème fraîche and the seasoning shines though. Sweet pineapple enhances the salty, tangy, savory flavors. Whether you love pineapple and ham or haven't jumped on that flavor bandwagon yet, give this recipe a try.

Lamb Meatball & Orzo Soup
Serves 4 to 6

1 large leek, white and light green parts diced and rinsed (about 2 cups)

1 small fennel bulb, diced (about 2 cups), fronds reserved for garnish

1 large shallot, diced (about ½ cup)

1 pound ground lamb

1 egg

½ cup dried bread crumbs

2½ tablespoons Hidden Cove Lemon Garlic Blend, divided

1½ teaspoons kosher salt, divided

1 tablespoon olive oil

2 medium carrots, sliced into thin rounds (about 1 cup)

¼ teaspoon coarse ground black pepper

8 cups chicken broth

¾ cup uncooked orzo pasta

3 ounces spinach leaves (about 2 cups)

1 lemon, sliced

For the meatballs: Preheat oven to 400 degrees and line 2 baking sheets with parchment paper. Set half of the diced leek, fennel, and shallot aside in a small bowl. Place remaining half in a food processor and pulse until finely chopped. Transfer the pulsed veggies to a large bowl and add ground lamb, egg, bread crumbs, 1½ tablespoons of the Hidden Cove, and 1 teaspoon of the salt. Mix with hands until thoroughly combined. Form into tablespoon sized meatballs and place on prepared baking sheets. (You should end up with about 40 meatballs.) Bake for 25 minutes, turning meatballs over halfway through to brown evenly. Transfer meatballs to a paper towel-lined platter.

For the soup: Heat oil over medium heat in a Dutch oven or soup pot. Add reserved diced veggies along with carrots, pepper, and remaining ½ teaspoon salt. Cook until softened, stirring frequently, 8 to 10 minutes. Add broth and remaining 1 tablespoon Hidden Cove and bring to a boil. Add meatballs and orzo and simmer for 10 minutes. Remove from heat and stir in spinach just before serving; spinach will wilt slightly. Serve warm garnished with chopped fennel fronds and a slice of lemon.

HIDDEN COVE LEMON GARLIC BLEND

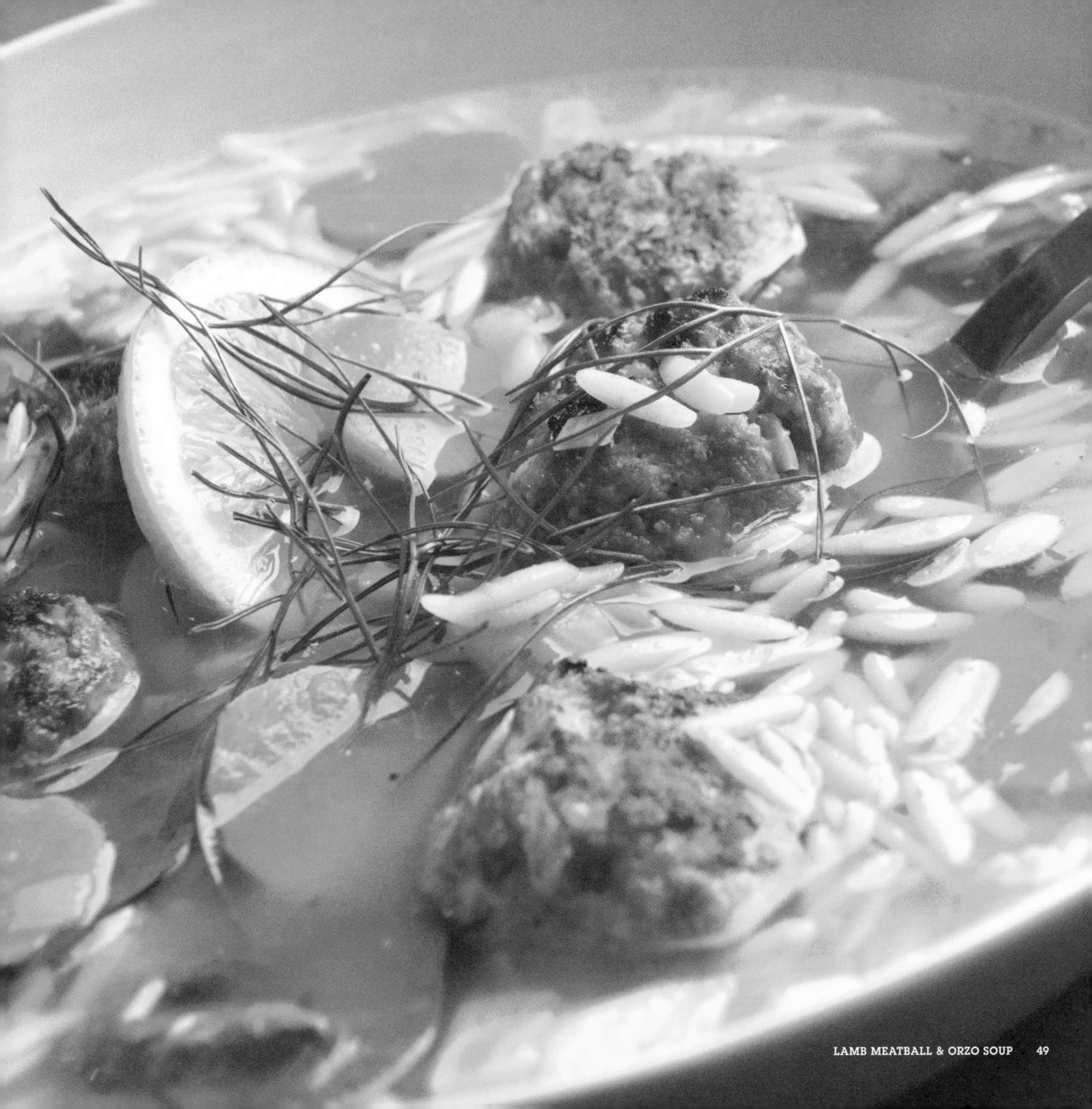

"My family enjoyed the many layers of flavor in this dish; we especially loved all of the fruit combined with the crunchy almonds. We liked it even better the next day as chilled leftovers." ~ Treena Milano, Berthoud, CO

Harvest Couscous
Serves 4 to 6

- 2 tablespoons plus ¼ cup olive oil, divided
- 1 large shallot, diced (about ½ cup)
- ¼ teaspoon dehydrated minced garlic (or 2 cloves garlic, minced)
- 2 cups uncooked Israeli (or pearl) couscous
- 2½ cups water
- 2 tablespoons Hidden Cove Lemon Garlic Blend, divided
- 1 teaspoon kosher salt, divided
- ½ cup sliced almonds
- 3 tablespoons apple juice
- 3 tablespoons orange juice
- 3 tablespoons lemon juice
- 1 green apple, diced
- 1 red Anjou or Red Bartlett pear, diced
- ¾ cup dried cherries
- 2 tablespoons diced crystallized ginger
- ½ cup packed fresh mint leaves, half chopped for salad and half kept whole for garnish

Heat 2 tablespoons of the oil in a large skillet over medium heat. Add shallots and cook until translucent, about 5 minutes. Stir in garlic and cook for 1 more minute. Add couscous and stir continuously to toast; couscous will turn an even golden color in about 5 minutes. Continue stirring while slowly pouring in the water. Cook, stirring occasionally, until water evaporates and couscous is al dente, about 8 minutes. Remove from heat and stir in 1 tablespoon of the Hidden Cove and ½ teaspoon of the salt. Set aside to cool. Gently fluff with a fork to break up any clumps.

In a small skillet over medium-high heat, toast almonds until golden, stirring continuously, about 5 minutes. Set aside to cool.

In a large bowl, whisk apple, orange, and lemon juices with remaining 1 tablespoon Hidden Cove and remaining ½ teaspoon salt. Continue whisking while drizzling in remaining ¼ cup oil until mixture is thick and smooth. Fold in cooked couscous, toasted almonds, apples, pears, cherries, ginger, and chopped mint leaves. Garnish with whole mint leaves before serving. Can be served at room temperature or chilled.

Ham & Asparagus Frittata with Pineapple Cream Sauce

Serves 4 to 6

For the frittata:

8 eggs

½ cup crème fraîche

¼ cup heavy cream

1 tablespoon plus 1 teaspoon Hidden Cove Lemon Garlic Blend

½ teaspoon coarse ground black pepper

½ cup shredded Mozzarella cheese

1 cup ½-inch diced cooked ham (4 to 6 ounces)

1 cup 1-inch pieces asparagus (6 to 8 spears)

2 tablespoons olive oil

For the sauce:

1 (8-ounce) can crushed pineapple, drained (or ½ cup minced fresh pineapple)

½ cup crème fraîche

¼ cup heavy cream

1 teaspoon Hidden Cove Lemon Garlic Blend

½ lemon, zest grated and juiced

2 tablespoons chopped fresh chives

Crème fraîche yields a fluffier frittata. Sour cream works as a substitute but yields a slightly denser texture.

For the frittata: In a large bowl, whisk eggs with crème fraîche, cream, 1 tablespoon of the Hidden Cove, and the pepper. In a separate bowl, toss cheese with remaining 1 teaspoon Hidden Cove. Heat oil over medium-high heat in a 10-inch oven safe nonstick or cast iron skillet. Add ham and asparagus and cook until asparagus is just tender and most of the liquid in the pan has evaporated, 5 to 7 minutes. Turn heat down to medium-low and pour in egg mixture. Cook undisturbed until eggs start to set and edges start pulling away from sides of pan, 10 to 15 minutes. While eggs cook, preheat broiler. When eggs are fully set around the edges and middle is not yet set, sprinkle seasoned cheese across the top. Place skillet under broiler for 3 to 5 minutes until eggs are set and top is golden. Let frittata cool for 5 to 10 minutes before serving.

For the sauce: Sauté pineapple in a small saucepan over medium-high heat, stirring frequently, until it releases most of its juice and just starts to brown, 5 to 7 minutes. Reduce heat to medium-low and stir in crème fraîche, cream, and Hidden Cove. Gently simmer, stirring often, until sauce thickens slightly, about 5 minutes. Remove from heat and stir in lemon zest and juice.

To serve: Cut frittata into slices and serve with a generous dollop of sauce and garnish with chives.

HIDDEN COVE LEMON GARLIC BLEND

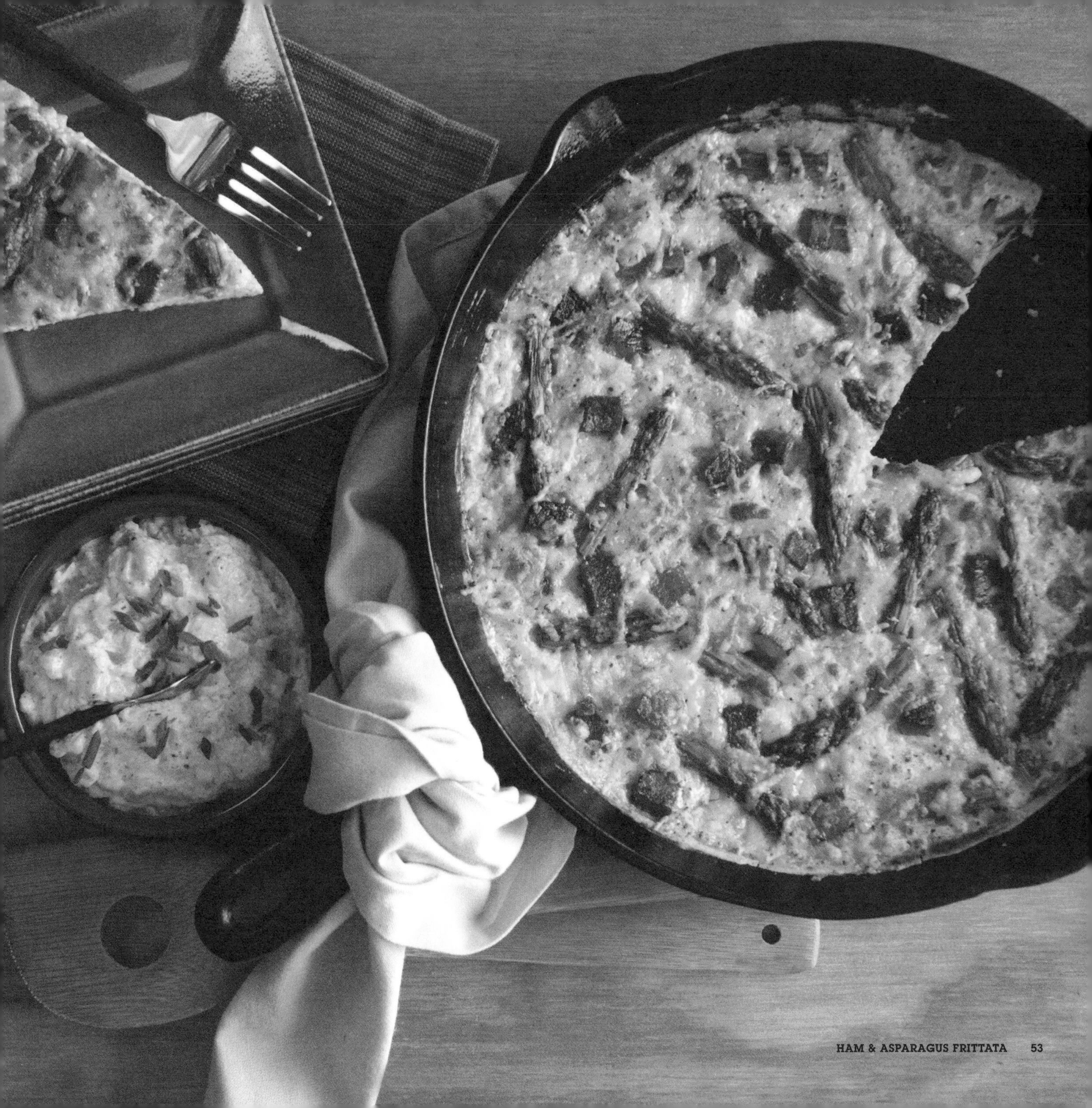

Savory
Spice Shop®

Homestead Seasoning

Purchase
Date: Net   2.5oz
                        Weight: 70g
6295 S. Main St., Aurora, CO - (303) 680-2117
www.savoryspiceshop.com

HOMESTEAD SEASONING

HOMESTEAD SEASONING

Inspired by classic flavors and essential spices, Homestead contains paprika, garlic, salt, pepper, sugar, honey powder, onion, coriander, mustard, shallots, parsley, fenugreek, turmeric, mace, thyme, lemon peel, cumin, ginger, cayenne, arrowroot, cinnamon, anise, cloves, and cardamom. With the sun-dried fragrance of paprika, earthy seeds, sharp garlic, and a hint of cinnamon sweetness, the seemingly unending flavor makes this an all-purpose seasoning.

Stephanie's Recipe Tasting Notes

Homemade Gravlax: Whether you top a slice of rye or a boiled, baked bagel with this cured salmon, one bite transports you to a New York deli. It's surprisingly easy to make gravlax (or lox) at home. While it requires a few days of planning, the finished product can be stored in the fridge for about a week or in the freezer for even longer. The seasoning enhances the salmon's natural flavor and the accompanying cheese spread boosts the spice-infused deliciousness of the gravlax.

Sweet & Golden Potato Salad: Potato salad should, first and foremost, be easy to make. Once I saw how easy this recipe was, and that it could be made ahead, I was enticed. The taste and texture has me hooked: sweet and tangy, creamy with a crunch, mild yet well-seasoned. Radishes, which I'd never had in potato salad, add a welcome crunch and subtle peppery taste. The end result is a dish complex enough to please an adult palate but sweet and creamy enough to keep the kids happy, too.

French Onion Roast on Toast: This recipe could have been called "The Marriage of a Perfectly Seasoned Roast and Rich Oniony Broth Just Might Change Your Life." Unfortunately, that title didn't fit the page. The smooth, rich broth of French onion soup is accented by sweet caramelized onions. The complex seasoning is simply perfect on the roast and the presentation elevates rustic comfort food to the status of modern classic. The first bite is sure to elicit an uncontrollable, "mmmmm!"

"I never would have thought to put Homestead on salmon; it was awesome! I've always wanted to try curing salmon and this was an easy recipe to start with. The Hungarian spread was excellent on a cracker with chopped egg, too." ~ Laura Shute, Corona del Mar, CA

Homemade Gravlax with Hungarian Cheese Spread
Serves 4 to 6

For the gravlax:

1 (8- to 10-ounce) salmon fillet

2 tablespoons Homestead Seasoning

2 tablespoons kosher salt

4 tablespoons sugar

For the spread:

½ cup unsalted butter, softened

4 ounces cream cheese, softened

1 clove garlic, finely minced

1 tablespoon finely minced yellow or red onion

1 tablespoon chopped dill pickle

½ teaspoon finely minced anchovies or anchovy paste (optional, see Note)

1 tablespoon Homestead Seasoning

Toasted bread or crackers for serving

Starting with a very fresh piece of salmon, somewhat even in thickness, is the key to successful curing. If omitting the anchovy from the spread, use ¼ teaspoon kosher salt instead.

For the gravlax: Rinse salmon fillet, pat dry with paper towels, and place in a gallon-size zip top storage bag. In a small bowl, whisk Homestead with salt and sugar. Add seasoning mixture to the bag and use your hands to spread mixture over salmon, covering it evenly and thoroughly. (There will be extra seasoning that falls off the salmon; leave it in the bag.) Seal the bag, place it between two plates and weight it with a heavy can set on top. (The weight will help the salmon release its moisture.) Place it in the refrigerator for three days to cure. Turn the curing salmon over in the bag twice a day, carefully redistributing the liquid and seasoning each time so the salmon remains fully covered. (This will help the salmon cure evenly.) The salmon will be ready to eat on the third day. (It should be firmer than sushi but not jerky-like. Thin ends of the fillet will be more "well done" and the thicker middle will be more "rare.")

Remove salmon and discard the bag with remaining liquid. Use a paper towel to gently absorb any excess liquid on the salmon. To serve, slice the fillet on the diagonal into very thin pieces, sliding it off the skin. Store wrapped in plastic in a sealed container in the refrigerator. Use within one week or freeze for up to two months.

For the spread: Place butter, cream cheese, garlic, onion, pickle, anchovy, and Homestead in a food processor and blend until smooth. (Alternatively, blend by hand in a bowl with a ➤➤

→ wooden spoon until well combined.) Cover and refrigerate until ready to use. Before serving, let spread sit at room temperature for about 15 minutes to soften slightly. Spread over toasted bread or crackers, top with thin slices of gravlax and serve.

Sweet & Golden Potato Salad

Serves 6 to 8

2 cups peeled, 1-inch cubed sweet potatoes or yams (1 to 2)

2 cups peeled, 1-inch cubed Yukon Gold potatoes (2 to 3)

½ cup mayonnaise

¼ cup apple cider vinegar

2 tablespoons olive oil

1 tablespoon Homestead Seasoning

½ medium red onion, diced

2 medium carrots, peeled into thin strips lengthwise, strips cut into bite-size pieces

1 bunch radishes (10 to 12), sliced into thin rounds

½ cup finely chopped fresh parsley, divided

Kosher salt and coarse ground black pepper

Place cubed potatoes in a large pot and add enough cold water to cover potatoes plus 3 inches. Bring to a boil. Check potatoes at 15 minutes; you want them to be fork tender but firm, not falling apart. Continue to check in 5-minute increments until done. The sweet potatoes will be slightly more tender than the Yukon Gold. Drain, transfer to a large bowl and cool to room temperature.

Meanwhile, prepare dressing by whisking mayonnaise, vinegar, and oil with Homestead until completely combined.

Gently fold dressing into cooled potatoes. Then fold in onions, carrots, radishes, and half of the parsley. Stir in salt and pepper to taste. Cover and refrigerate for at least an hour. Just before serving, sprinkle remaining parsley on top.

HOMESTEAD SEASONING

"This roast has fantastic flavor and the dish is very rich compared to your classic French onion soup. Sprinkling the extra Homestead over each serving at the end is a must. I can see this being a regular meal for our weekend family gatherings." ~ Michael Sandhoff, Aurora, CO

French Onion Roast on Toast
Serves 4 to 6

- 3 pounds boneless chuck roast
- 2 tablespoons unsalted butter
- 3 tablespoons olive oil, divided
- 2 tablespoons Homestead Seasoning, divided
- 2 teaspoons kosher salt, divided
- 5 medium yellow onions, French cut (see Note)
- 4 cups beef or chicken broth (or water)
- 1 baguette
- 2 cloves garlic, smashed
- 6 ounces Gruyere cheese, thinly sliced into strips

To French cut an onion: Trim off stem and root ends; turn trimmed onion onto one of its flat ends; cut it in half lengthwise; remove thin paper layer; and slice it from end to end, with the knife always angled toward the center of the onion, to create long thin strips.

Remove roast from refrigerator about an hour before starting, to bring it to room temperature. Rinse roast, pat it dry, trim any visible fat and season with 1 tablespoon of the Homestead and 1 teaspoon of the salt. Heat butter and 1 tablespoon of the oil over medium-low heat in a Dutch oven or heavy-bottomed soup pot until butter is melted. Increase heat to medium-high, add roast to the pot and brown each side, 3 to 5 minutes per side. Remove roast from pot and set aside.

Reduce heat to medium and scrape bottom of pot to release browned beef bits. Add onions, sprinkle with a pinch of salt and cook for 10 minutes, covered. Uncover and cook for another 30 to 45 minutes, stirring frequently, to caramelize and brown the onions. Nestle the browned roast on top of the onions and pour in broth. Bring to a boil then reduce to a low simmer. Cover and cook until fork tender, about 3 hours. (Check every half an hour or so to make sure the broth remains at a low simmer.) Remove roast from pot and let it rest on a cutting board, tented with foil, for 10 minutes. While roast rests, continue to simmer onions and broth to reduce into a thin sauce, about 15 minutes. Season sauce to taste with additional Homestead and salt.

Meanwhile, preheat oven to 375 degrees and line a baking sheet with parchment paper. Slice the baguette diagonally into 1-inch thick pieces. In a small bowl, mix together remaining 2 tablespoons olive oil with garlic. Brush bread slices with »→

→ oil-garlic mixture and bake for about 12 minutes, turning slices over halfway through, until golden brown and toasted. To serve, slice roast against the grain into ½- to 1-inch thick pieces. Lay a slice of toasted bread in the bottom of a shallow bowl. Layer with slices of roast and cheese. Top with a heaping pile of caramelized onions from the sauce. Then spoon extra sauce into the bottom of the bowl. Garnish with a sprinkle of additional Homestead. Serve with remaining toasted bread to sop up the sauce.

PARIS CHEESE SPRINKLE

Inspired by a classic French bouquet garni herb blend, Paris contains Romano cheese powder, garlic, salt, dill, green onion, basil, chives, tarragon, chervil, parsley, and pepper. The herbs in this blend give it a vivid hue and a garden fresh scent. Salty cheese, buttery herbs, and a hint of onion and garlic add flavor without overwhelming the other ingredients in a recipe.

Stephanie's Recipe Tasting Notes

Dill Pickle Roll Ups: A plate of roll ups is always my dad's contribution to parties and it's almost always the first plate emptied. This roll up recipe is wrapped (literally) around the distinctive flavor of pickle. With very few ingredients, each is crucial: briny pickle, salty and savory meat, herbed cheese, fresh parsley, and familiarly spiced bread. These roll ups have a crowd-pleasing quality and were quickly snatched up by our resident tasters.

Parisian Gnocchi: These pillowy gnocchi, infused with herbs and cheese, can simply be described as delicious. The recipe may look a bit intimidating but don't be deceived, although long it is fairly easy. The French technique yields bites that are more airy than their potato-based counterparts; pan frying them adds a crispy exterior. Roasted yellow tomato pesto, which can be made ahead, is a new spin on a classic sauce. The finished dish is decadent and hearty, with bits of savory sausage, brightened by the tomato pesto.

Peppercorn & Cheese Crusted Steak: Improving already good steak is a monumental, some might even say impossible, task. The beauty of this recipe lies in two simple flavors: pepper and cheese. Crusting the steak with coarsely cracked peppercorns adds texture and complexity. Buttery and roasted, the cheesy herbed topping entices you to take another bite. The topping would be good on other proteins as well as sides like potatoes or asparagus. Pair with the Roasted Brussels Caesar Salad (one of our Bonus Side Dish recipes) to create an unbeatable steakhouse dinner.

Dill Pickle Roll Ups

Makes 30 roll ups

8 ounces whipped cream cheese

2 tablespoons Paris Cheese Sprinkle

10 slices light or dark rye bread
(or combination)

20 (3-inch) sprigs flat-leaf parsley

10 deli thin salami slices (e.g.
genoa, capicola, soppressata,
or combination)

10 baby dill pickles, 2½ to 3 inches
in length and relatively straight

To make croutons with the leftover bread crusts: Dice the crusts; toss with 1 tablespoon olive oil and 1 tablespoon Paris; and bake in a 375-degree oven for 12 to 15 minutes.

In a small bowl, thoroughly mix together the cream cheese and Paris and set aside. Trim crusts off each slice of bread to create a rectangle shape approximately 3 inches by 4½ inches in size. Using a rolling pin, roll each bread slice flat on both sides.

Spread a semi-thin layer of flavored cream cheese on each slice of flattened bread. Top each with two sprigs of parsley and one slice of salami, then spread another slightly thicker layer of cream cheese over salami. Lay 1 pickle so it parallels the short end of a bread slice and carefully roll it up away from you. Gently press to seal the roll; the cream cheese should act as the glue to keep the roll together.

Using a bread knife, cut each roll into three equal size segments. (You will get better looking slices if you carefully wipe the knife clean of cream cheese before slicing the next roll.) Serve cold or at room temperature.

Parisian Gnocchi with Sausage and Yellow Tomato Pesto

Serves 4 to 6

For the gnocchi:

1 cup water

1 teaspoon kosher salt

6 tablespoons unsalted butter, divided

1 cup flour

3 eggs

2½ tablespoons Paris Cheese Sprinkle

8 ounces ground turkey sausage, pinched into ¾-inch pieces

Shaved or shredded Parmesan for garnishing

For the yellow tomato pesto:

1¼ pounds yellow cherry tomatoes (about 4 cups)

1 tablespoon olive oil

¼ cup pine nuts

¼ teaspoon dehydrated minced garlic (or 2 cloves garlic, minced)

1 cup packed fresh parsley sprigs

1 teaspoon kosher salt, plus more to taste

1 teaspoon sugar, plus more to taste

¼ teaspoon crushed red pepper flakes

½ lemon, zest grated

1 cup vegetable broth

⅓ cup dry white wine (e.g. Sauvignon Blanc)

This recipe follows the traditional method for making Parisian-style gnocchi, which is made from pâte à choux, the same dough used for making profiteroles. The gnocchi can be made ahead, either to the dough or boiled gnocchi stage, and refrigerated for up to 2 days in an airtight container.

For the gnocchi: Bring water, salt, and 3 tablespoons of the butter to a boil in a small saucepan over high heat. Reduce heat to medium, add flour and vigorously mix with a wooden spoon until thick dough pulls away from the sides of the pan, about 1 minute. Keep stirring and cook for another minute to dry out the dough. Transfer to a medium bowl to cool for 5 minutes. Meanwhile, bring a large pot of salted water to a boil and prepare a large bowl of ice water to set near the stovetop.

Using a wooden spoon, beat one egg into cooled dough until fully incorporated; dough will be slightly lumpy. Beat in Paris and another egg until well blended, then beat in last egg. Dough should be smooth and have a slight sheen. »→

→ Reduce pot of boiling water to a simmer. Transfer dough to a zip top storage bag, pressing it into one of the bag's corners. Snip off corner to create a ½-inch opening. Lightly spray kitchen shears with nonstick cooking spray; these will be used to cut the dough. Hold bag above simmering water with one hand and gently squeeze dough out of the opening. Cut dough into 1- to 1½-inch pieces as it comes out and let the pieces drop into the water. Cut as many pieces as you can in one minute then set dough aside. Gently stir simmering dough to prevent pieces from sticking together. After all pieces rise to the surface, simmer for 2 more minutes. With a slotted spoon, transfer gnocchi to prepared ice bath for a minute to stop the cooking, then transfer to a paper towel-lined cooling rack and gently pat dry. Repeat process until all dough is cooked.

For the yellow tomato pesto: Preheat oven to 400 degrees. Place tomatoes on a baking sheet, toss with oil and season with a little salt. Roast for 40 to 45 minutes until tomatoes are a deep golden brown color; set aside to cool. Meanwhile, toast pine nuts and garlic in a small skillet over medium-high heat until aromatic and lightly browned, 3 to 5 minutes, stirring or gently tossing to prevent burning; set aside to cool. Place roasted tomatoes, toasted pine nut mixture, and parsley in a food processor. Add salt, sugar, crushed red pepper flakes, and lemon zest. Process for 1 to 2 minutes until mixture is smooth. Season with additional salt and sugar to taste. Transfer to a medium skillet or saucepan. Whisk in broth and wine. Bring to a low simmer and cook, stirring occasionally, until sauce reduces and thickens slightly, about 10 minutes.

To finish: Melt remaining 3 tablespoons butter in a large nonstick skillet over medium-high heat. Add sausage and gnocchi. Cook undisturbed until browned on one side, 4 to 6 minutes, then toss to brown the other side, another 4 to 6 minutes. Gently stir in pesto and heat through, 3 to 4 minutes. Serve warm topped with Parmesan.

Peppercorn & Cheese Crusted Steak

Serves 4

- 2 tablespoons Four Corners Peppercorn Blend (or other whole peppercorns, see Note)

- 4 (4- to 6-ounce) filet mignon or tri-tip steaks

- ½ teaspoon kosher salt, plus more for seasoning

- ¼ cup unsalted butter, softened

- ¼ cup Panko bread crumbs

- 2 scallions, white and green parts minced

- 2 tablespoons Paris Cheese Sprinkle

- 2 tablespoons grated Parmesan cheese

- Coarse ground black pepper

- 1 tablespoon vegetable oil

Four Corners contains pink peppercorns, which are related to cashews and may produce an allergic response in people with allergies to tree nuts. Serve with the Roasted Brussels Caesar Salad on page 95.

For the steak: Place peppercorns in a gallon-size zip top storage bag and seal. Use a rolling pin or meat pounder to roughly crack peppercorns. Add steaks and ½ teaspoon of the salt to the bag. Roll steaks around, pressing cracked peppercorns into each steak until coated on all sides. Refrigerate for at least 30 minutes.

For the topping: Thoroughly combine butter, bread crumbs, scallions, Paris, and Parmesan. Add salt and pepper to taste. On a sheet of parchment or wax paper, shape scoops of the mixture into four ¼-inch thick flattened disks that will fit over the entire top of each steak. (Eyeball the steaks to determine approximate size disks you'll need; you may end up with leftover topping depending on size of steaks.) Leaving disks of topping on the paper, refrigerate for at least 30 minutes.

To cook: Preheat broiler and remove the steaks and topping from the refrigerator. Heat vegetable oil in a cast iron skillet (or similar ovenproof skillet) over high heat. Reduce heat to medium-high and add steaks. For a medium-rare to medium steak, sear for 5 to 6 minutes on one side then flip and cook for 2 to 3 more minutes. Working quickly, place a disk of topping on each steak and put the skillet under the broiler until topping is lightly browned with some green still showing, about 3 minutes. Immediately transfer steaks to a platter and let rest for 5 to 10 minutes before serving.

PARK HILL
MAPLE & SPICE PEPPER

Inspired by the dual flavors of sweet and spicy, Park Hill contains maple sugar, sugar, pepper, coriander, turmeric, ginger, nutmeg, fenugreek, anise, cumin, cinnamon, mustard, mace, cardamom, and green onion. This sweet blend is tempered by the warmth of spices commonly found in curry blends. The bold, complex seasoning adds a sweet and buttery quality when used with olive oil, salmon, and other natural fats.

Stephanie's Recipe Tasting Notes

Salmon Salad Cakes: While the individual components of this recipe are good, it's a dish that gets even better as you build it. The creamy dressing, sweet and slightly tart, is delectable by itself and would make a good condiment for other dishes. The salmon salad portion of the recipe could be served cold. But if you like crab cakes, you'll love making these into seared salmon cakes. Finish with crisp cucumber or greens and an extra drizzle of that scrumptious dressing for a light summer meal.

Acorn Squash Salad Rounds: I could sip this dressing. Okay, that's an exaggeration, but it really is fantastic. The sweet and spicy flavors of the seasoning are balanced by bright orange juice and rich olive oil. Substantial but not heavy, the dish is fresh and beautifully composed – as if plated in a fancy restaurant rather than prepared at home. As an added benefit, this recipe gives you a great way to use the whole squash rather than tossing the seeds in the garbage or compost.

Maple Waffles: I have an affinity for multi-purpose recipes. Breakfast for dinner or dessert for breakfast? Yes, please! This recipe fits the bill. The waffles have a pleasant warmth from the curry-inspired spices and the peach chutney is a balance of sweet and savory. Have it with orange juice or tea and a side of bacon, call it breakfast. Have it with a beer and a pork chop, call it dinner. Have it with wine or coffee and vanilla ice cream, call it dessert.

Salmon Salad Cakes

Makes 12 to 16 cakes

1 (12-ounce) salmon fillet

½ teaspoon olive oil

1 tablespoon plus 1 teaspoon Park Hill Maple & Spice Pepper

½ cup mayonnaise

½ cup full fat Greek yogurt

1 teaspoon lemon juice

1 tablespoon plus 1 teaspoon chopped fresh chives

1 tablespoon chopped capers

½ teaspoon onion salt

¼ cup dried bread crumbs

¼ cup plus 1 tablespoon finely diced red bell pepper

1 to 2 tablespoons canola oil

1 large cucumber, sliced into ⅛- to ¼-inch rounds

You can substitute the cooked salmon fillet with canned or smoked salmon. For a cold version of the salad, simply leave out the bread crumbs and stop before preparing the cakes. Toss with dressing to taste and serve on cucumber rounds or over mixed greens.

For the salmon salad: Preheat oven to 450 degrees. Lay salmon skin side down on a parchment-lined baking sheet. Lightly rub olive oil over salmon and sprinkle with 1 teaspoon of the Park Hill to coat the fillet. Bake for 15 minutes. Let cool completely on the baking sheet. Prepare a dressing by mixing remaining 1 tablespoon Park Hill with mayonnaise, yogurt, lemon juice, 1 tablespoon of the chives, capers, and onion salt. Once salmon is cool, pull out any small bones and remove the skin. Hold the fillet with one fork and use another fork to pull against the flesh, creating small flakes. Place salmon flakes in a medium bowl. Fold in half of the dressing then stir in bread crumbs and bell peppers. Reserve remaining dressing for topping.

For the cakes: Heat 1 tablespoon of the canola oil in a nonstick skillet over medium-high heat. Take 1 tablespoon of salmon salad at a time and form it into ¼- to ½-inch thick patties that are about the same diameter as your cucumber rounds. Place several at a time in the skillet and cook 2 to 3 minutes per side, or until each side is nicely browned. Transfer to a paper towel-lined plate and cook remaining cakes, adding additional oil to skillet as necessary.

To assemble: Lay each cake on a cucumber slice and top with at least ¼ to ½ teaspoon remaining dressing. Arrange on a serving platter and garnish with remaining 1 teaspoon chopped chives and 1 tablespoon diced red bell peppers. Serve immediately.

PARK HILL MAPLE & SPICE PEPPER

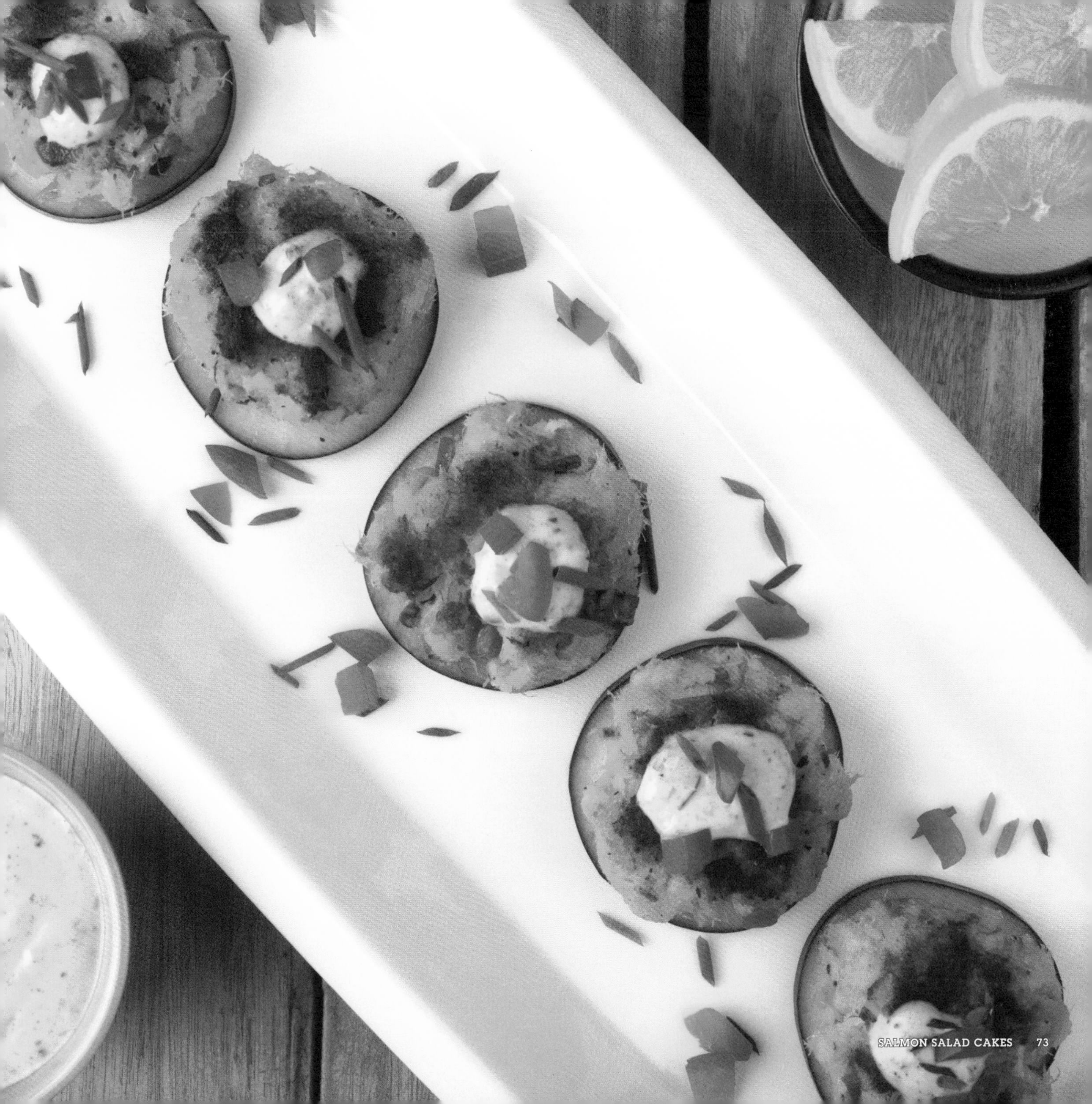

Acorn Squash Salad Rounds

Serves 4 to 6

½ cup olive oil, divided

1½ teaspoons grated orange zest, divided

1 large acorn squash (2 to 3 pounds)

3 teaspoons Park Hill Maple & Spice Pepper, divided

¾ teaspoon kosher salt, divided

¼ cup juice from zested orange

1 tablespoon apple cider vinegar

2 heaping cups mixed salad greens (about 3 ounces)

2 ounces feta cheese, crumbled

Whisk ¼ cup of the oil with 1 teaspoon of the orange zest and set aside. Preheat oven to 300 degrees. Cut squash in half horizontally (between the two ends, rather than end-to-end). Scoop out seeds and rinse, removing any pulp so seeds are clean. Lay seeds on a paper towel-lined plate and pat dry. Toss seeds with half of the oil-orange mixture and lay them in a single layer on a parchment-lined baking sheet. Bake for 15 minutes. Remove from oven, transfer to a small bowl and toss with 1 teaspoon of the Park Hill and ¼ teaspoon of the salt.

Increase oven temperature to 400 degrees. Carefully slice each squash half into ¾- to 1-inch rounds to yield 4 total slices. (If slicing full rounds is difficult, cut each in half again and slice into half moons.) Set slices on the same parchment paper-lined baking sheet used for the seeds. Brush the squash slices with remaining oil-orange mixture. Using 1 teaspoon of the Park Hill, generously sprinkle the slices with seasoning. Bake just until fork tender, 20 to 25 minutes. Sprinkle ¼ teaspoon of the salt across the slices when they come out of oven. Transfer to salad plates to cool.

Prepare dressing by whisking orange juice and vinegar with remaining ¼ cup oil, ½ teaspoon orange zest, 1 teaspoon Park Hill, and ¼ teaspoon salt. In a large bowl, toss greens with 1 tablespoon of the dressing. Divide dressed greens evenly atop the squash rounds, nestling greens into the opening. Sprinkle with toasted squash seeds and feta. Serve remaining dressing alongside the salad.

PARK HILL MAPLE & SPICE PEPPER

74

*"This recipe was a little adventurous for me, but I'm glad I made it.
It's both sweet and savory, and the onion in the compote is surprisingly delicate.
A terrific brunch dish!"* ~ Doug Johnson, Normal, IL

Maple Waffles with Bourbon Peach Chutney
Serves 6 to 8

For the chutney:

4 just ripe peaches (or about 24 frozen peach slices, defrosted)

2 tablespoons plus 1 teaspoon bourbon

2 tablespoons olive oil

1 medium yellow onion, diced

1 tablespoon Park Hill Maple & Spice Pepper

¼ cup maple syrup

½ cup raisins

½ teaspoon kosher salt

3 sprigs fresh thyme, leaves removed from stems

For the waffles:

2 cups flour

2 teaspoons baking powder

1 teaspoon baking soda

½ teaspoon kosher salt

2 tablespoons Park Hill Maple & Spice Pepper

2 cups buttermilk

3 eggs

¼ cup vegetable oil

2 tablespoons maple syrup

1½ teaspoons maple or vanilla extract

The chutney can be made ahead and will keep in a sealed glass jar in the refrigerator for several weeks. Turn the waffle batter into pancake batter by thinning it out with an additional ¼ to ½ cup buttermilk.

For the chutney: Preheat grill to high and make sure grates are well oiled. (Alternatively, use a grill pan or skillet on the stovetop over medium-high heat.) Halve or quarter peaches and remove pits. Toss peaches with 2 tablespoons of the bourbon and let sit for 10 minutes. Reserving bourbon, transfer peaches to grill and cook for 2 to 3 minutes per side or until each side has nice grill marks. Transfer grilled peaches back to bowl of bourbon and let cool. Chop peaches into 1-inch pieces and place them back in the bowl.

Heat oil in a large skillet over medium-high heat. Add onions and cook until just softened but not translucent, 4 to 6 minutes. Stir in Park Hill and cook for another minute. Reduce heat to low and stir in maple syrup and raisins. Add grilled peach and bourbon mixture. Cook for about 10 minutes, stirring occasionally, until raisins are plump and peaches are soft but still hold their shape. Stir in remaining 1 teaspoon bourbon and cook for another minute. Remove from heat and stir in salt and thyme leaves.

For the waffles: Sift flour, baking powder, baking soda, and salt into a large bowl, then add Park Hill. In a separate bowl, whisk buttermilk, eggs, oil, maple syrup, and extract. Fold wet ingredients into dry until smooth. Preheat waffle iron. Pour ½ cup batter at a time into waffle iron and cook according to manufacturer's instructions. Serve warm topped with chutney.

PARK HILL MAPLE & SPICE PEPPER

PLATTE RIVER RIB RUB

Inspired by the perfect rack of ribs, Platte River contains paprika, salt, brown sugar, pepper, chili powder, garlic, onion, nutmeg, and hickory smoke flavoring. Roasted and toasted spices heighten the smoky notes of this barbeque-inspired blend and are balanced by the essential flavors of salty and sweet.

Stephanie's Recipe Tasting Notes

Potato Parsnip Soup: Barbeque seasoning in a vegan soup may sound crazy, but it's actually brilliant. Wafting up from the pot is a smoky, sweet, spicy aroma. The pinch of salt activated my taste buds and made me eager for more of this velvety soup. Hearty but not heavy, earthy parsnip is balanced by the nuttiness of pumpkin seeds and sweet, smoky seasoning. The spiced pumpkin seeds are a great snack, so I'd recommend making a double batch!

Schnitzel Bites: These bites are the perfect DIY fried snack. They can easily be cut into larger dinner portions and served with a salad. The roasted red pepper topping has a slightly sweet and acidic flavor with a hint of smoke, which is a delicious counterpoint to the pork. The compote is versatile – add to grilled cheese sandwiches, spread on crackers, or use as a topping for fish. A fun and surprising garnish, the capers burst and resemble flowers when fried.

Strawberry BBQ Skewers: Marinated grilled skewers, strawberry barbeque sauce, and a side of lemony quinoa makes a perfect al fresco dinner. Syrupy balsamic vinegar, salty soy sauce, and smoky seasoning create a flavorful marinade that pairs perfectly with sweet roasted strawberries and the slight heat of chiles. For quick assembly, make the sauce the day before and warm it up when you start grilling the skewers. Lemon Poppy Seed Quinoa (one of our Bonus Side Dish recipes) rounds out the meal with just a kiss of tart citrus. These skewers have become one of my summer staples.

"This soup is even better the second day after the flavors have had a chance to meld. And we loved the pumpkin seed garnish; we ended up making many batches because they couldn't survive on our counter." ~ Laura Chambers, Homewood, IL

Potato Parsnip Soup with Toasted Pumpkin Seeds
Serves 4 to 6

For the soup:

2 tablespoons olive oil

3 large leeks, white and light green parts sliced and rinsed

1 pound parsnips (3 to 4), peeled and chopped into 1-inch pieces

1 pound russet potatoes (2 to 3), peeled and chopped into 1-inch pieces

2 tablespoons Platte River Rib Rub

¼ teaspoon kosher salt

⅛ teaspoon coarse ground black pepper

4 cups vegetable broth

For the pumpkin seeds:

½ cup raw shelled pumpkin seeds

¼ teaspoon olive oil

¼ teaspoon Platte River Rib Rub

This recipe yields a thick soup. For a thinner soup, add additional broth or water before pureeing it. This soup also freezes well.

For the soup: Heat oil over medium-low heat in a Dutch oven or soup pot. Add leeks, parsnips, and potatoes and cook for 10 minutes, stirring occasionally. Add Platte River, salt, and pepper. Stir until vegetables are coated with seasoning. Cook for 2 more minutes then stir in broth and bring to a boil. Reduce heat and simmer, covered, for 20 minutes or until vegetables fall apart when you poke them with a fork. Remove from heat and use an immersion or stand blender to puree until smooth. Gently reheat over medium-low heat. Serve warm garnished with the toasted pumpkin seeds.

For the pumpkin seeds: While soup cooks, toast pumpkin seeds in a large skillet over medium-high heat for 5 to 7 minutes or until seeds are fragrant and start to brown and puff up. Stir frequently to avoid burning. Transfer toasted seeds to a small bowl and toss with olive oil and Platte River. Set aside to cool. These keep for up to a week in an airtight container at room temperature.

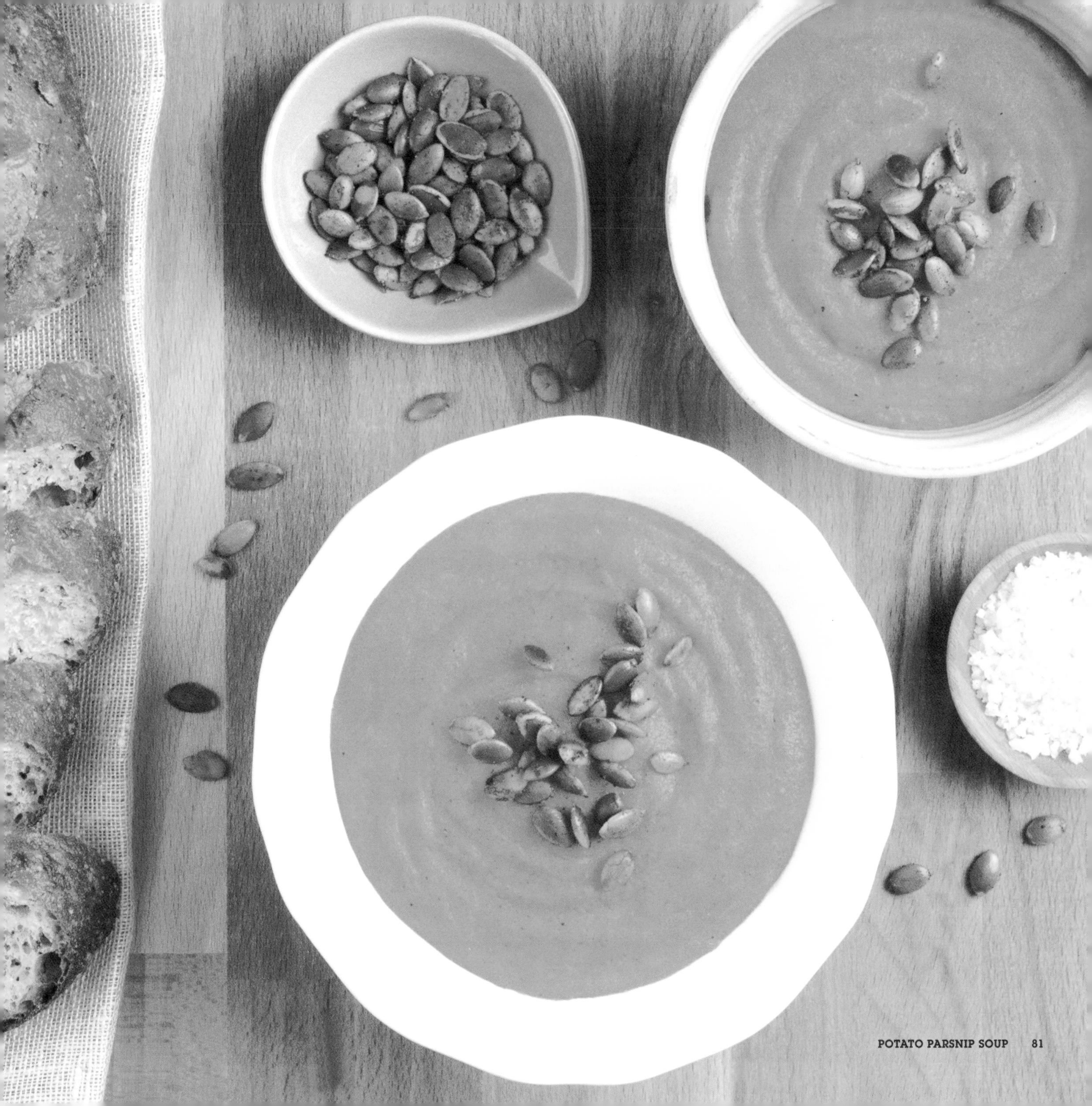

"While there are a lot of pieces to this recipe, it's easy to make. It works for a weeknight meal, it's fun for kids, and it's great as passed hors d'oeuvres for a party. You could also skip the bites and make four large schnitzels as a main meal." ~ Elizabeth Woessner, Denver, CO

Schnitzel Bites with Roasted Red Pepper Compote
Makes 16 to 20 bites

For the schnitzel:

4 thin cut boneless pork loin chops
(¾ to 1 pound total)

1 tablespoon plus 1 teaspoon
Platte River Rib Rub, divided

Vegetable oil for frying

½ cup flour

2 eggs

2 cups Panko bread crumbs,
finely ground in a food processor

2 tablespoons heavy cream

1 (4-ounce) jar capers,
drained and patted dry

¼ cup chopped fresh herbs
(e.g. dill, chives, parsley)

For the compote:

2 tablespoons unsalted butter

2 large shallots, halved and
thinly sliced (about 1 cup)

2 cloves garlic, minced

1 tablespoon Platte River Rib Rub

1 (12-ounce) jar roasted red peppers,
drained and diced

⅛ teaspoon kosher salt

1 lemon, juiced

Buying thin cut pork chops makes it easier to pound out chops to desired thinness. Fry schnitzel while compote cooks so the components are done about the same time.

For the schnitzel: Place pork chops in a quart-size zip top storage bag (or between 2 sheets of wax paper) one at a time and pound each to between ⅛- and ¼-inch thickness. (The thinner the better, but you don't want the meat to break apart.) Divide 1 tablespoon of the Platte River between the 4 chops and sprinkle both sides evenly with seasoning. Transfer to a plate or sealable container, cover and refrigerate for at least 2 hours or up to overnight. When ready to prepare the schnitzel, remove chops from the refrigerator and let them come to room temperature. Fill a deep skillet or Dutch oven with at least 1 inch of oil. Heat oil to 350 degrees over medium-high heat. Create an assembly line next to the stovetop with separate bowls of the flour, eggs, and bread crumbs. Lightly whisk cream into the eggs. Cut marinated pork chops into about 2-inch pieces; you should get 4 to 6 pieces from each chop. Lightly dredge each piece in flour, then egg, then bread crumbs. Fry 4 to 6 pieces at a time for 1 to 2 minutes per side or until golden brown. Transfer to a paper towel-lined plate. Once all pieces are fried, carefully add capers to the hot oil to fry for about a minute. (Wet capers will cause oil to splatter, so use caution.) Remove capers with a fine mesh strainer or slotted spoon and set on a paper towel-lined plate.

For the compote: Melt butter in a small saucepan over medium-low heat. Stir in shallots and garlic and cook, partially covered, until shallots soften and start to brown and caramelize, 10 to 15 minutes. Keep heat at medium-low to low to avoid burning. ⇢

→ Stir in 1 tablespoon of the Platte River. Add roasted red peppers and salt. Stir in lemon juice and cook for 3 to 5 more minutes until most of the liquid evaporates. Remove from heat and cover until ready to assemble schnitzel bites.

To assemble the bites: Place fried pork pieces on a platter and top each with a small spoonful of compote. Sprinkle with the fried capers and fresh herbs. Finish by sprinkling remaining 1 teaspoon Platte River across the platter of bites. Serve warm or at room temperature.

Strawberry BBQ Skewers

Serves 4 to 6

For the skewers:

¼ cup balsamic vinegar

¼ cup olive oil

2 cloves garlic, smashed

2 tablespoons dark brown sugar

2 tablespoons soy sauce

1 tablespoon Platte River Rib Rub

½ teaspoon coarse ground black pepper

2 pounds flank steak (or boneless, skinless chicken tenderloins)

For the strawberry BBQ sauce:

1 pound strawberries, hulled

¼ large red onion, sliced

2 cloves garlic, smashed

1 small serrano or jalapeño chile, halved and seeded

¼ cup dark brown sugar

2 tablespoons balsamic vinegar

1 tablespoon Platte River Rib Rub

1½ teaspoons tomato powder (or 1 tablespoon tomato paste)

The skewers can also be cooked in a 425-degree oven on a foil-lined baking sheet for 5 to 10 minutes, depending on the meat. Serve with the Lemon Poppy Seed Quinoa on page 97.

For the skewers: Whisk vinegar and oil with garlic, brown sugar, soy sauce, Platte River, and pepper. Pour into a gallon-size zip top bag. Slice steak against the grain into ¼-inch thick strips and place strips in bag with marinade. Seal and shake to coat steak with marinade. Refrigerate for 2 to 4 hours. (If using chicken tenderloins, marinate for 30 minutes to 2 hours.) Preheat grill to medium-high. (If using wooden skewers, soak in water for at least 1 hour to avoid burning on the grill.) Thread each steak slice onto a skewer. Grill skewers until meat reaches desired doneness, about 2 minutes per side for medium-rare. (Chicken tenders will take longer to cook through depending on thickness.) Just before skewers come off the grill, brush with strawberry BBQ sauce. Serve with additional sauce for dipping.

For the strawberry BBQ sauce: Preheat oven to 450 degrees. Line a baking sheet with parchment paper and scatter strawberries (cut large ones in half), onions, garlic, and chile on top. Roast for 15 to 20 minutes until strawberries begin to release their juices. Transfer roasted fruit and vegetables to a food processor. Add brown sugar, vinegar, Platte River, and tomato powder and blend until smooth. Transfer to a small saucepan and bring to a simmer. Stirring occasionally, maintain a gentle simmer until sauce has reduced to desired consistency, 5 to 10 minutes for a thinner sauce or 20 to 30 minutes for a thicker sauce. Remove from heat and allow sauce to cool. Cover and refrigerate until ready to use. Sauce will keep in the refrigerator for up to a week.

ZANZIBAR CURRY POWDER

Inspired by an African breakfast curry, Zanzibar contains lemon peel, garlic, salt, ginger, onion, allspice, parsley, white pepper, sugar, fenugreek, turmeric, mace, black pepper, thyme, coriander, cumin, cayenne, arrowroot, cinnamon, anise, cloves, and cardamom. The combination of spices is both exotic and familiar. Experiment with this curry in some of your favorite recipes or try something new and different.

Stephanie's Recipe Tasting Notes

Beer Battered Fish Tacos: For years I was convinced that fish tacos were a restaurant dish – nearly impossible to make well in your own home. I couldn't have been more wrong. These little gems are surprisingly easy to make and pack a flavor punch. The addition of curry to the crema adds a slight heat to the tangy lime sauce – don't skimp on this creamy condiment! Tangy pickled onions and crunchy cabbage are a nice contrast to the perfectly fried bits of fish. With so many flavors, everyone at the table can customize their own taco.

Chicken Biryani: Each bite of this dish is different, enticing me to experience the variety of flavors. In one bite, you taste sweet apricots or raisins and in the next, mild curry artfully seasons a piece of chicken. Crunchy pumpkin seeds and nuts are a textural contrast to the toothsome rice, and parsley lends its distinctive freshness. This is a great weeknight meal because you can improvise a bit with the ingredients you already have in your pantry. Making this the day before allows the flavors time to meld and the result is even more delicious.

Mango Coconut Sherbet: I'm a self-proclaimed ice cream aficionado but even for me a curry sherbet was unexpected. This recipe is as delightful as it is surprising. As is the case with some curries, the heat in the blend will continue to build, tempered here by the icy mango and the creaminess of the coconut milk. The lime juice is essential, as it brightens the flavor with a welcome acidity. Scoop the sherbet into a bowl or a sweet and crunchy sugar cone. You can even turn it into a tropical float by adding cream soda or flavored sparkling water.

Beer Battered Fish Tacos with Curry Crema
Serves 6 to 8

For the pickled onions:

1 cup apple cider vinegar

1 teaspoon sugar

1 teaspoon kosher salt

½ large red onion, thinly sliced

For the curry crema:

½ cup full fat Greek yogurt

½ cup mayonnaise

1 lime, juiced

1½ tablespoons Zanzibar Curry Powder

¼ teaspoon kosher salt

For the beer battered fish:

1 pound tilapia (or other firm white fish)

1½ tablespoons Zanzibar Curry Powder, divided

1½ cups flour, divided

2 tablespoons cornstarch

1 teaspoon baking powder

1 teaspoon kosher salt

1 cup (8 ounces) light beer

1 egg, beaten

Vegetable oil for frying

For the tacos:

12 to 16 corn tortillas

4 to 6 sweet mini bell peppers

2 cups shredded red cabbage

1 cup fresh cilantro leaves

For the pickled onions: Whisk vinegar, sugar, and salt until sugar and salt are dissolved. Place onions in a glass jar and pour in vinegar mixture to cover onions. Seal and refrigerate for at least 1 hour.

For the curry crema: Whisk yogurt, mayonnaise, lime juice, Zanzibar, and salt. Cover and refrigerate until ready to assemble tacos.

For the beer battered fish: Cut fish into 2-inch long pieces. Toss with ½ tablespoon of the Zanzibar and set aside. In a large bowl, whisk 1 cup of the flour with cornstarch, baking powder, salt, and remaining 1 tablespoon Zanzibar. Stir in beer and egg; batter should be wet but still lumpy. Fill a deep skillet or Dutch oven with at least 1 inch of vegetable oil and heat over medium-high to 350 degrees. Create an assembly line next to the stovetop to include a plate each of seasoned fish pieces, remaining ½ cup flour, and batter. Lightly dredge each piece of fish in the flour then coat with batter. Fry fish in batches for about 2 minutes per side or until golden brown. Transfer to a paper towel-lined plate.

For the tacos: Heat corn tortillas in batches in a large skillet over medium heat for about 30 seconds per side and stack on a serving plate. Slice mini bell peppers into thin rounds. Arrange fried fish (whole or cut pieces), pickled onions, curry crema, mini bell peppers, cabbage, and cilantro in separate serving bowls. Serve family style so everyone can build tacos to taste.

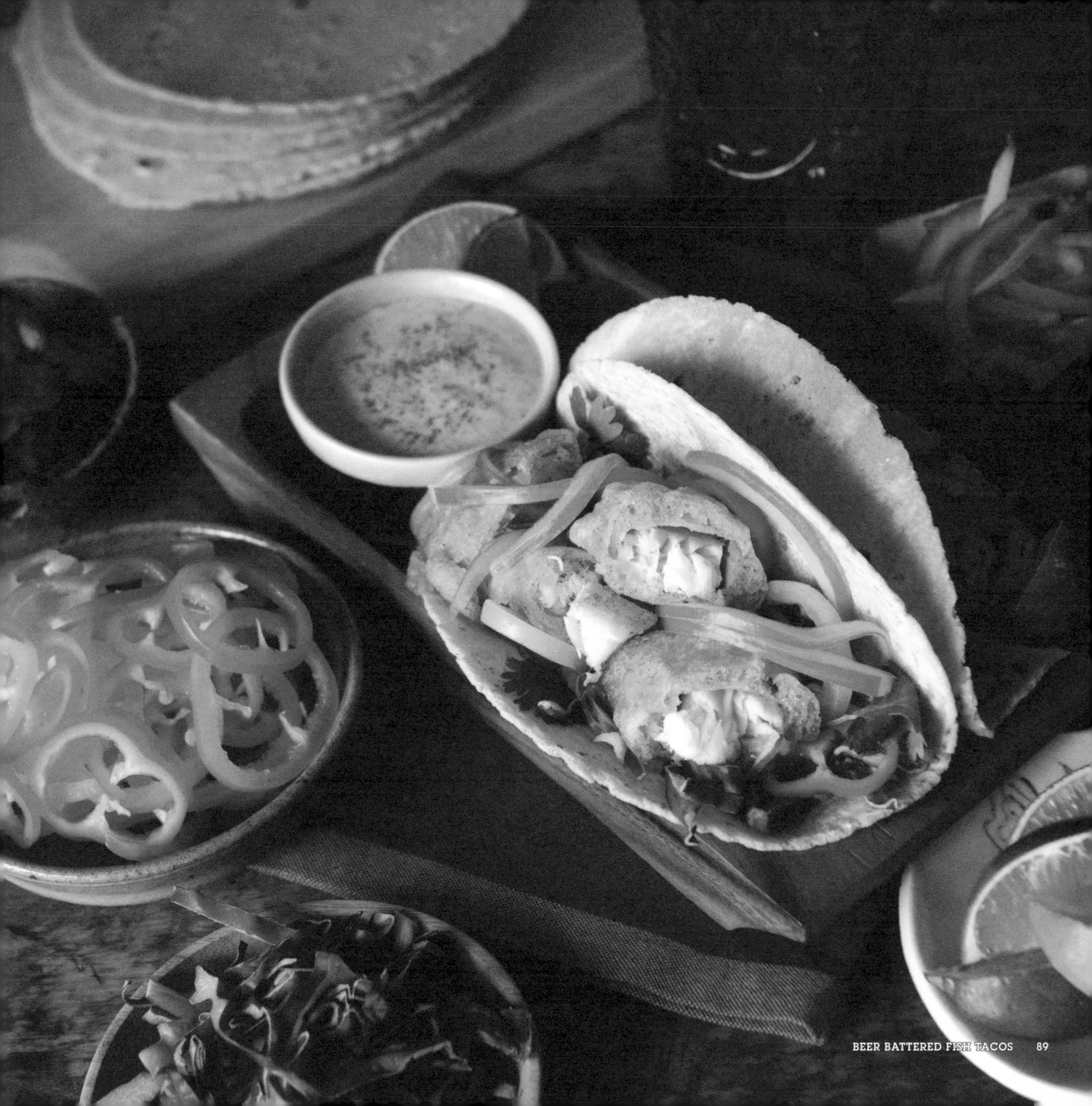

Chicken Biryani

Serves 4 to 6

- 1 pound boneless, skinless chicken thighs or breasts
- 2 tablespoons Zanzibar Curry Powder, divided
- 1 teaspoon sea salt, divided
- 1 tablespoon olive oil
- 3 tablespoons unsalted butter or ghee
- 1 medium yellow onion, diced (about 1 cup)
- 1 cup basmati rice, rinsed
- 1 to 2 small tomatoes, chopped (about ½ to 1 cup)
- 2 cups chicken broth
- ½ cup chopped dried fruit (e.g. dates, apricots, raisins, currants)
- ¼ cup raw shelled pumpkin seeds
- ¼ cup chopped or sliced almonds
- 1 tablespoon chopped fresh parsley
- 1 lemon, juiced

Cut chicken into bite-size cubes and toss with 1 tablespoon of the Zanzibar and ½ teaspoon of the salt. Heat oil over medium heat in Dutch oven or large sauté pan. Add chicken and sauté until lightly browned and cooked through, 5 to 7 minutes. Transfer to a clean bowl and cover with foil.

In the same pan, melt butter over medium heat. Add onions and sauté until softened and browned, 7 to 8 minutes, scraping up any browned bits from the chicken. Stir in rice and remaining 1 tablespoon Zanzibar and cook for another 2 minutes. Stir in tomatoes, broth, and remaining ½ teaspoon salt. Bring to a boil then reduce to a simmer and cook, covered, for 20 minutes. Remove from heat and let stand for 10 minutes before removing lid.

Fluff the rice with a fork then fold in cooked chicken, dried fruit, pumpkin seeds, almonds, and parsley until combined. Season with lemon juice to taste. Serve warm.

ZANZIBAR CURRY POWDER

90

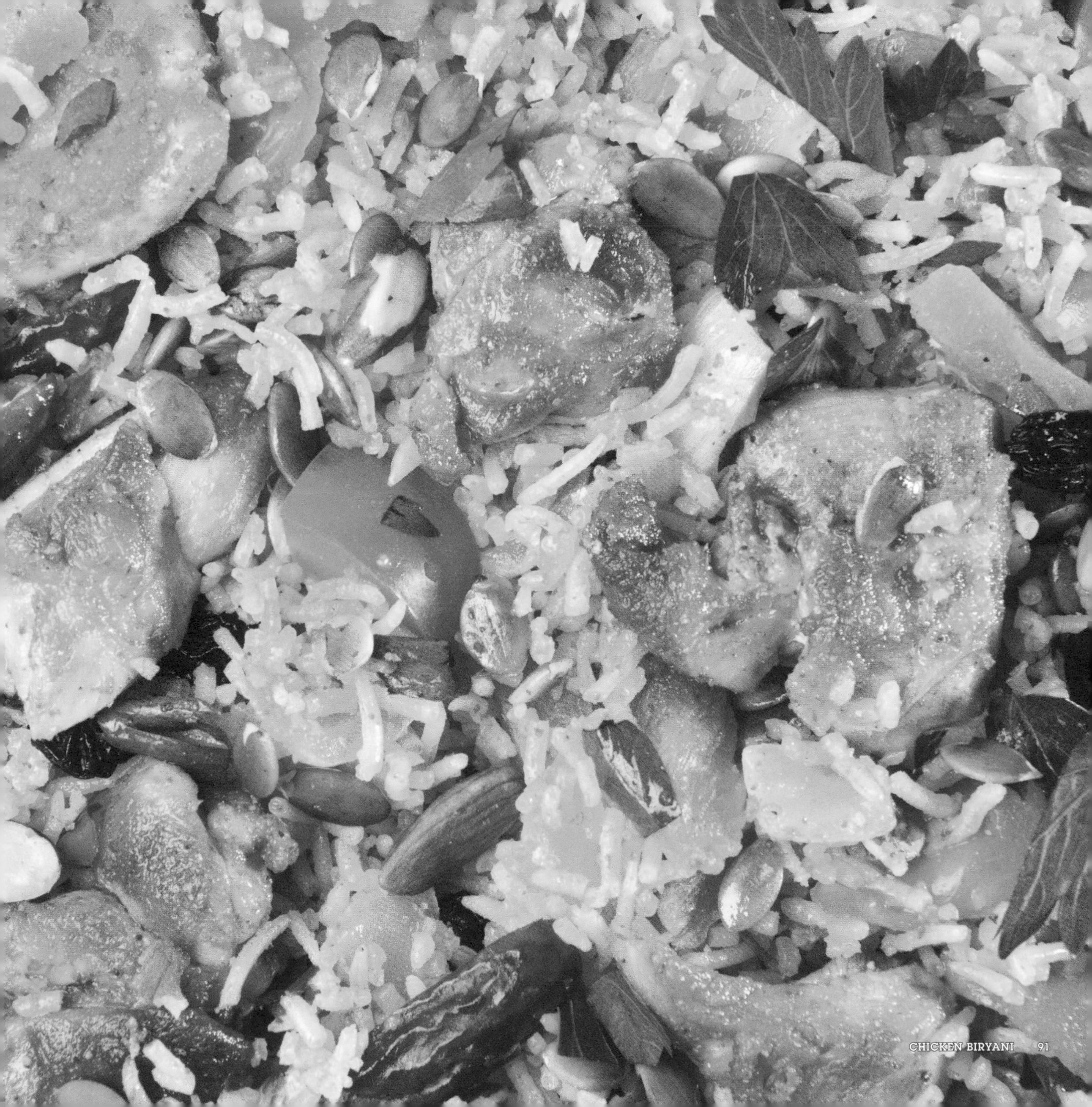

Mango Coconut Sherbet

Makes 1 quart

- 2 (13.5-ounce) cans full fat coconut milk

- 1 cup sugar

- 2 teaspoons Zanzibar Curry Powder

- 2 large ripe mangoes, peeled, pitted, and cut into chunks (about 3 cups)

- 2 limes, zest grated and juiced

This recipe requires an ice cream maker. Frozen mango chunks can be used in place of fresh; defrost first for best results.

Whisk coconut milk, sugar, and Zanzibar in a medium saucepan over medium heat until sugar is dissolved, about 3 minutes. Remove from heat and transfer to a sealable container to cool. Puree mango in a blender or food processor until smooth; transfer to a sealable container. Cover and refrigerate both the coconut milk mixture and mango puree for at least 3 hours or up to overnight; you want them to be well chilled before processing in an ice cream maker.

When ready to prepare sherbet, whisk together chilled coconut milk mixture and mango puree with lime zest and juice. Pour mixture into an ice cream maker and freeze according to manufacturer's directions. Serve immediately for a soft sherbet, or transfer to a sealable container and freeze until firm before serving.

Bonus Side Dishes

⁂

While developing the recipes in *Spice to Plate*, we created a few flavorful accompaniments. These Bonus Side Dishes showcase popular spices (mentioned in the Spice Rack on page 10) that accent the ten blends featured in this book. We included these recipes when sending the Peppercorn & Cheese Crusted Steak, Chorizo Glazed BBQ Chicken, and Strawberry BBQ Skewers to our recipe testers. They agreed that these side dishes completed those meals and should be included. In the recipes that follow, the main dish pairing is listed as the serving suggestion. Together, these main and bonus side dishes create a satisfying and "Savory" meal.

"This is a nice portable dish for picnics or parties because it can be served cold or at room temperature. The kids even loved it! It would also make a simple main dish with a crisp glass of white wine and some crostini in lieu of the bread crumbs." ~ The Bach Family, Denver, CO

Roasted Brussels Caesar Salad

Serves 4 to 6

For the Brussels sprouts:

2 pounds Brussels sprouts

1 tablespoon unsalted butter

1 tablespoon olive oil

4 cloves garlic, sliced ⅛ to ¼-inch thick

2 teaspoons smoked sweet or hot Spanish paprika

¼ teaspoon kosher salt

For the dressing and salad:

4 tablespoons heavy cream

1 tablespoon red wine vinegar

2 teaspoons Dijon mustard

1 clove garlic, minced

1 teaspoon minced anchovies or anchovy paste (optional)

2 tablespoons grated Parmesan cheese

1 lemon, zest grated and juiced

½ cup olive oil

½ teaspoon smoked sweet or hot Spanish paprika

Kosher salt and coarse ground black pepper

¾ cup Panko bread crumbs (toasted, optional)

Serve with the Peppercorn & Cheese Crusted Steak on page 68.

For the Brussels sprouts: Preheat oven to 425 degrees. Trim about ¼ inch off of the root end of the sprouts then cut lengthwise into thirds. Save any loose leaves that fall off the sprouts. Place butter and oil in the middle of a roasting pan or rimmed baking sheet. Place pan in the oven and allow oil and butter to melt for about 3 minutes. Add sprouts, any extra leaves, and garlic slices to the pan and toss with tongs to lightly coat with melted butter and oil. Sprinkle with paprika and salt and place back in the oven to roast for 20 to 30 minutes, tossing every 5 minutes; you should end up with some crisp leaves and caramelized, browned larger pieces. Transfer to a large bowl to cool.

For the dressing and salad: Combine cream, vinegar, Dijon, garlic, anchovies, Parmesan, lemon zest, and juice. Whisk at an even pace while slowly drizzling in the olive oil; the dressing should become smooth and creamy. Stir in paprika and season with salt and pepper to taste. Toss roasted sprouts with dressing and chill in the refrigerator for at least an hour or up to overnight. Fold in bread crumbs just before serving.

Festival Fritters with Honey Butter
Makes 20 to 30 fritters

For the fritters:

2 cups flour, plus more for rolling dough

¼ cup cornmeal

3 tablespoons sugar

1 heaping teaspoon baking powder

½ teaspoon ground ginger

½ teaspoon crushed red pepper flakes

¼ teaspoon ground Saigon cassia cinnamon

¼ teaspoon kosher salt

2 tablespoons finely chopped fresh chives

3 tablespoons unsalted butter, cold, cubed

1 cup whole milk

Vegetable or canola oil for frying

For the honey butter:

¼ cup (1 stick) unsalted butter, softened

4 tablespoons honey

Serve with the Chorizo Glazed BBQ Chicken on page 44.

For the fritters: In a large mixing bowl, combine flour, cornmeal, sugar, baking powder, ginger, crushed red pepper, cinnamon, salt, and chives. Work butter into flour mixture with your fingers until fully incorporated and mixture looks like fine bread crumbs. Stir in milk to form a pliable dough. Form dough into 1-inch balls; you should end up with 20 to 30 balls. On a lightly floured surface, roll each ball out into a rope about ½-inch thick by 6 inches long; twist rope into a simple knot. Repeat with remaining dough.

In a medium saucepan, heat at least 1 inch of oil to 350 degrees. Cook up to 4 dough knots at a time in the oil until golden brown, about 2 minutes per side. Using a slotted spoon, transfer fritters to a paper towel-lined rack; cover to keep warm. Serve with honey butter.

For the honey butter: Whisk softened butter with honey until smooth and serve.

Lemon Poppy Seed Quinoa

Serves 4 to 6

1 cup quinoa

2 cups water

¼ cup olive oil

1 lemon, juiced

2 tablespoons minced red onion

1 tablespoon sugar

1 tablespoon Dutch blue poppy seeds

½ teaspoon sea salt

¼ teaspoon coarse ground black pepper

1 cup packed spinach leaves, roughly chopped

1 cup sliced strawberries

¼ cup slivered almonds (optional)

Serve with the Strawberry BBQ Skewers on page 84.

Rinse quinoa and place in a medium saucepan with water. Bring to a boil then reduce heat to low, cover and cook until water is absorbed, 15 to 20 minutes. Remove from heat and let sit, covered, another 5 minutes. Remove cover, fluff quinoa with a fork and let cool.

In a large salad bowl, whisk oil, lemon juice, onion, sugar, poppy seeds, salt, and pepper. Add cooled quinoa and spinach and toss to coat with dressing. Fold in strawberry slices and slivered almonds (if using). Cover and refrigerate until ready to serve. Serve cold or at room temperature.

ACKNOWLEDGEMENTS

In the homegrown spirit of Savory Spice Shop, we took a grassroots approach to publishing this cookbook. Our internal cookbook crew created and produced all of the recipes, content, design, and photography. We also asked family and friends of Savory to volunteer their time and energy for photography, editing, and recipe testing. We truly could not have completed this cookbook without their help. As they say, "It takes a village!" Savory's "village" for this project includes not only those listed here, but also those behind-the-scenes who went above and beyond to offer support: unofficial taste testers, enthusiastic dishwashers, patient family members (who had to eat the same meals over and over!), friends who were willing to give their opinions (solicited or not!), and many others.

A special thank you to:

Kaeli Sandhoff ~ *Photography Contributions:* Kaeli and her husband, Michael, own the Savory Spice Shop in Aurora, CO. Kaeli's other passion, besides spices, is photography. She specializes in gorgeous family photos at www.kaelijophotography.com. For this book, Kaeli helped us capture beautiful images of the Savory environment in the store, in the blending room, and in the test kitchen.

Mary Cardas ~ *Content Editing:* Mary owns the Savory Spice Shop in Palm Desert, CA. Mary is as meticulous about running her spice business as she is about writing and editing. Mary's attention to every little detail made her the perfect choice for helping us dot every "i" and cross every "t" in this book.

Allison Saunders ~ *Recipe Proofing:* A longtime friend and fan of Savory's, Allison graciously volunteered to lend her cookbook production experience. Allison's culinary training has led her down a path of professional recipe development, testing, and editing for several culinary and cookbook projects. We were lucky to have her seasoned eyes glancing over our final recipes from her home in New York, NY.

Our Moms ~ *Content Proofing:* Isn't it typical of Mom to be there at the last minute, right when you need her most? That's how cookbook contributors Janet, Stephanie, and Suzanne feel about their moms Paula Chambers, Jackie Bullen, and Cheryl Klein. These wonderful, supportive women dropped everything to be the last sets of eyes to help proof the final cookbook, in its entirety, just before it went to press. Thanks, Moms!

Spice to Plate Recipe Testers

The 33 recipes in this cookbook were tested in the home kitchens of more than 50 volunteers across the country, from Savory Spice Shop owners and spice merchants to loyal customers and supportive family members. Every recipe was edited, tweaked, and sometimes styled for photographs based on recipe tester feedback. These testers made our recipes better in ways we never would have imagined.

Savory Spice Shop owners:

Stephanie & Jason Birn ~ *Encinitas/San Diego, CA*

Able & Kari Blakley ~ *Oklahoma City, OK*

Dan Hayward ~ *Boulder, CO*

Clayton Kile ~ *Friendly Center/Greensboro, NC*

Susan Kirkpatrick ~ *Fort Collins, CO*

Amy MacCabe ~ *South End/Charlotte, NC*

Hollie, David, Alexis & Mia Rollins ~ *Franklin, TN*

Michael & Kaeli Sandhoff ~ *Southlands/Aurora, CO*

Laura Shute & Randy Morton ~ *Corona del Mar/ Newport Beach, CA & The OC Mix/Costa Mesa, CA*

David & Darice Trout ~ *Lincoln Square/Chicago, IL*

Savory Spice Shop merchants, customers, friends, and family:

Debbie Ager ~ *Parker, CO*

Chris Bendig Andrews ~ *Franklin, TN*

The Bach Family ~ *Denver, CO*

Peggy Bamford ~ *Lutz, FL*

Joe Bamford ~ *Lutz, FL*

Frankie Barrett ~ *Denver, CO*

The Bolin Family ~ *Centennial, CO*

Debi Blake ~ *Franklin, TN*

Shara Brandon ~ *Chicago, IL*

Pam Braverman ~ *Colorado Springs, CO*

Kerry Brown ~ *Atlanta, GA*

Candie Cain & Family ~ *Alma, CO*

Laura & Dan Chambers ~ *Homewood, IL*

Chad Ciferri ~ *Westfield, NJ*

Amanda Faison ~ *Denver, CO*

Brooke Franklin ~ *Littleton, CO*

Rebekah & Matt Giaraffa ~ *Denver, CO*

Liz Henry & Nastassia Cruz ~ *Aguadilla, PR*

Anthony D. Jones ~ *Charlotte, NC*

Doug & Kristen Johnson ~ *Normal, IL*

Kelly Landgraf ~ *Centennial, CO*

Amanda Lee ~ *Bend, OR*

Sandy Marvin ~ *Englewood, CO*

Treena & Dave Milano ~ *Berthoud, CO*

Bonnie Milzer ~ *Denver, CO*

Lia Moran ~ *Denver, CO*

Marge Moran ~ *Centennial, CO*

Kortney Morrisson ~ *Englewood, CO*

Erin Mousel ~ *Lincoln, NE*

Courtney O'Rourke ~ *Denver, CO*

Tenashia Pharms ~ *Charlotte, NC*

Emilie Rogers ~ *Greensboro, NC*

Elly Cooke Ross ~ *Charlotte, NC*

Jack Stephens ~ *Oakland, CA*

Shalom C. Stephens & Mike Bober ~ *Manchester Ctr., VT*

Ashley Stricker ~ *Greensboro, NC*

Kathy VanPeursem ~ *Denver, CO*

Samanthia Waltjen & Austin Kingsley ~ *Bend, OR*

Elaine Willoughby ~ *Winthrop, ME*

Elizabeth Woessner ~ *Denver, CO*

Rachel Zandlo ~ *Aurora, CO*

ABOUT THE COOKBOOK CREW

"You better have thick skin if you're going to work in the test kitchen!" ~ Our Mantra

As a company, Savory Spice Shop is fortunate to have many talented folks on staff. As a bonus, many of their talents revolve around creativity, both in the kitchen and beyond. Taking on the challenge of creating our first Savory Spice Shop cookbook has given us the opportunity to tap into all that talent. The crew we've put together is a fun bunch of adventurous home cooks who aren't afraid to come up with crazy ideas and fight for them. At the same time, they have thick enough skin to be true team players who can take constructive criticism and work together to produce the most flavorful results.

The process of writing these bios reinforced the fact that we have created a special working environment. They say, whoever "they" are, to never work with family or friends and to never get too close to your employees. We haven't followed those rules, which certainly brings extra challenges and obstacles. But when you find that sweet spot and truly make it work, no success is more fulfilling.

Stephanie Bullen ~ *Assistant Project Manager, Content Writer, Creative and Flavor Advisor:* Steph, as she is known around here, has been with Savory Spice Shop since 2008. She started as a seasonal part-time employee when Janet hired her on the spot, moved to full-time, and quickly rose to assistant manager of the Littleton, CO shop. It was clear that she could do a lot more, so with the development of the franchise system she was moved to "corporate" where she has had many roles.

Currently Steph wears a few different hats: providing technical support to our stores, helping launch new products, managing our compliance program, and writing articles about food and our products. We could just say she is versatile, but the reality is that she is highly valued. Steph cares about the details and always wants to get it right. No wonder Janet always boasts that she was the one to hire Steph!

Steph is an excellent writer, the obvious choice to write much of the content for this cookbook, but she could have easily been a recipe developer. She is a creative cook with an excellent palate – just check out her blog about cooking with alcohol at www.spiritedbites.wordpress.com! She has added real value (there's that word again) as a flavor advisor on this cookbook, which has helped everyone improve their final cookbook recipes.

Food travels ~ *"Every trip seems to include a few great meals. From a simple baguette sandwich in the fresh air of the Alps to suki (a soup dish cooked tableside) in Thailand, or from a salmon salad in Alaska to the perfect collards in North Carolina, every trip has a one-of-a-kind food memory."*

Top foodie related item on your bucket list ~ *"I would love to spend time learning how to cook authentic dishes from the people who know them best."*

Matthew Wallington ~ *Recipe Creator, Flavor Advisor:* Matt has been working at the original Savory Spice Shop (on Platte Street in Denver, CO) since 2010. He started part-time and quickly proved to be a customer-friendly food enthusiast and a loyal, hardworking employee. He moved his way up to management and is the perfect representation of Savory.

Matt has a great palate and is a natural in the kitchen; his true cooking gift is his expertise in desserts! He is regularly challenging boundaries with unexpected spices that not only taste good but also leave a wonderful, lasting memory. Those who are lucky enough to work with him are very often treated to one of his sweet creations. Those with a sweet tooth, beware: it is quite easy to get lost in the flavors and eat more than intended.

Matt may be the dessert king around here, but he also has a yin to his yang as he completed a culinary food nutrition program at the Nutrition Therapy Institute. Customers and employees alike are forever amazed by the food knowledge he possesses. If you want to know an obscure food fact, go ask Matt.

***Spice to Plate* seasonings** ~ Baker's Brew Coffee Spice and Zanzibar Curry Powder
Cooking philosophy ~ *"Butter is king!"*
Favorite food quote ~ *"When baking, follow directions. When cooking, go by your own taste."* – Laiko Bahrs

Suzanne Klein ~ *Project Manager, Recipe Editor, Creative and Art Direction, Food Styling, Recipe Creator, Flavor Advisor:* Suzanne works in and manages the Savory Spice Shop test kitchen, but has been a loyal customer and great friend of owners Janet and Mike since the beginning in 2004. Her life experiences (both at work and play), integrity, and dedication make her a highly valued employee who is truly respected.

Suzanne loves working with spices, but maybe not in a manner that one might expect. She is founder and owner of Zanitea, a tea company that specializes in tea blends, particularly teas blended with spices. She doesn't just make tea to drink, but also uses her culinary imagination to create wonderfully tasty tea-flavored dishes. We are not sure where she finds the time, but she also blogs about tea at www.teafoodie.com. When Suzanne is not working with spices or tea she enjoys pickling, fermenting, and making food from scratch, which is another reason she is the perfect person to manage our test kitchen.

Along with Janet and Mike, Suzanne and her significant other, Dan, are founding members of a gourmet club. When it's their turn to host, let's just say you know it's going to be a foodie night to remember!

Spice to Plate seasonings ~ Platte River Rib Rub and Barrier Reef Caribbean Style Seasoning

Favorite foodie resource aside from Savory ~ *"Borough Market in London is my favorite food market and overall food experience anywhere."*

Food travels ~ *"For my 40th birthday I dined at Thomas Keller's Per Se in New York. It was probably the most amazing meal I have had to date. I cried at the end of the meal (in a good way)."*

Mary Johnston ~ *Recipe Creator, Flavor Advisor:* Mary has been an employee of Savory Spice Shop since 2006, but as Mike's mom she has been a proud supporter even before the first shop opened. She has had many different jobs at Savory including working in both the Platte Street and the Littleton shops, fulfilling website orders, and cooking in the test kitchen.

She may be Mike's mom, but she has become a mother figure to the staff through her cooking. She makes her famous scones for any important meeting, and during the busy holiday season she prepares lunch every Wednesday for the entire staff at our production facility and corporate offices. Mary is loved and appreciated by the entire team not only for her food but for her generous spirit. That goes double for Mike and Janet, Rob (another son), and Charlie (her husband) – who all work together daily!

Mary's cooking style is what you'd expect from a mom, traditional and comfort driven. But the more she has worked with spices, the more exotic flavors have found their way into her cooking repertoire. If Mary is cooking for you, you're just as likely to have a Moroccan or Peruvian style dish as you are a Sunday pot roast or one of the many traditional Greek dishes she was brought up on.

Spice to Plate seasonings ~ Hidden Cove Lemon Garlic Blend and Park Hill Maple & Spice Pepper

Favorite cooking gadget ~ *"My microplane and my pasta maker."*

Food hobbies ~ *"I love collecting cookbooks and reading each one cover to cover!"*

Shantelle C. Stephens ~ *Recipe Creator, Flavor Advisor:* Shantelle has worked at the original Savory Spice Shop on Platte Street in Denver, CO since 2007. She worked side by side with owners Janet and Mike, becoming a true spice expert with the benefit of their training. Her hard work and her loyalty have made her a much loved member of the Savory Spice Shop family.

Shantelle is a gifted cook and even before joining the cookbook crew contributed recipes that have become customer favorites. She has been a foodie literally her whole life:

"Having parents who were into food and cooking, it was natural for me to pick it up. My mother would stick my high chair next to her in the kitchen and I took it all in. When I was seven I woke up early and made her breakfast… and it was good! I've enjoyed the satisfaction of feeding people from that day on. In addition, my palate was fostered from an early age. I ate whatever they did…hot spicy dishes, sausage, sushi, lobster, even little tastes of beer and wine."

How fitting that Shantelle is our resident brewer and often helps customers select an assortment of spices to flavor their own homebrews!

Spice to Plate seasonings ~ Homestead Seasoning and Bohemian Forest European Style Seasoning
Cooking philosophy ~ *"Learn technique, forget technique, riff."*
Favorite Savory Spice Shop seasoning ~ *"It is hard to pick one but I must say I love Capitol Hill Seasoning!"*

Tony Correa ~ *Graphic Designer, Photographer, Creative and Art Direction, Food Styling, Flavor Advisor:* Tony has been with Savory Spice Shop since 2009. However, as a long time close friend of Mike and Janet's he has been an involved, loyal supporter even before the first store opened.

His first major contribution was the design of the Savory logo. He came to Savory with 14 years of experience as the art director in the food and beverage industry. With that experience he has been entrusted as "Protector of the Brand," a job that he has done both effectively and graciously as a real team player. He has a big heart and a big laugh to match, which has endeared him to the entire Savory family.

Tony is a true foodie, but not the farm-to-table type. Although he is comfortable in any food environment, it's the hidden gems and longstanding dives that satisfy his foodie soul. "Will travel for food" is quite possibly Tony's motto in life; he has journeyed far and wide, from his homeland in the Philippines to a list of countries too long to mention. He and Mike have been digging up food treasures since they met back in the 1980s. Mike considers himself lucky to have such a wonderful friend and looks forward to many more opportunities to find tasty, and quite likely fatty, foodie joints with his ol' Chicago buddy.

Favorite food quote ~ *"There are no two finer words in the English language than 'encased meat' my friend."* – Hot Doug's, Chicago
Personal eating philosophy ~ *"Must be able to eat with your hands."* (He didn't specify as to whether or not that hand has a fork in it, but we suspect a fork would just get in the way!)

Janet C. Johnston ~ *Content Writer, Editing Assistant, Recipe Tester, Creative and Art Direction, Flavor Advisor:* Janet co-founded Savory Spice Shop with her husband Mike in 2004. While Mike is credited with most of the creative aspects, she is the soul and backbone of Savory. Mama bear, as she is often referred to, is always available to be a shoulder to cry on, in fact, she is likely to enjoy a good cry with you! We count ourselves fortunate that many of our employees stick around and grow with the company. One of the primary reasons is the positive culture that Janet has helped develop. Without her there is no doubt that Savory would not be the company that it is today.

Don't let all that syrupy stuff fool you – Janet is a headstrong business woman who will move you out of the way (gently) if you can't get the job done right. She is hungry to learn and has supreme organizational skills, which have been highly valuable to the nationwide system under which all Savory Spice Shops operate. Greatly influenced by her parents and family, she lets that grounded approach guide her in her daily life, which in turn influences many of the critical business decisions she faces on a regular basis.

As a foodie, Janet is ever evolving – mostly because Mike is always pushing her boundaries with the meals he creates at home. Her food passion is baking and she regularly steals Mike's thunder at their gourmet group when she closes out the meal with one of her mind-blowing desserts.

Favorite cooking gadget ~ *"Although not quite a gadget, a set of three nested stainless steel bowls that belonged to my grandma. I love them and don't bake anything without using at least one."*

Personal eating philosophy ~ *"Always take that 'no thank you' bite. You know, the one every finicky eater should take before politely saying 'no thank you.' Often times you'll discover that you like more than you think and begin to expand your culinary world!"*

Mike Johnston ~ *Cookbook Conceptualizer, Content Writer, Creative and Art Direction, Recipe Creator, Flavor Advisor:* Mike co-founded Savory Spice Shop with his wife Janet in 2004. He is truly the driving force and inspiration behind it. By combining his fine art background, love of food and cooking, unstoppable ambition, and a good amount of "street smarts," Mike has created a company that is exciting and forever evolving.

An artist at heart, the creative process has always inspired him, reflected in Mike's seasoning creations and in the overall look and feel of the Savory brand. His competitive business sense has led to new concepts which continue to move Savory into the future. These sometimes opposing traits have created the foundation for Savory's success.

Sometimes referred to as "the machine," Mike's fierce work ethic and tough love mentality may seem intimidating. He has a way of challenging those around him to do what they thought they couldn't, pushing them to be the best they can be. But the fact that he's never given a holiday party speech without shedding at least one tear or ended a work day without thanking his employees proves he's really a softy at heart.

Spice to Plate seasonings ~ Paris Cheese Sprinkle and Chimayo Chorizo Sausage Spice

Favorite dish to make at home ~ *"I make a pretty mean Pad Thai. What I love most about it is teaching guests in our kitchen, showing them just how easy and fun it is to make. We have tons of great photos with friends and family cooking this dish. Good times!"*

Top foodie related item on your bucket list ~ *"I'd love to get to the Oaxaca area in Mexico and learn how to make each of the seven moles in a traditional manner. Janet and I had this trip lined up, but had to cancel it when swine flu broke out back in 2009."*

INDEX